P9-DIW-782

The Wine Lover
Cooks with Wine

The Wine Lover
Cooks with Wine

GREAT RECIPES FOR THE

ESSENTIAL INGREDIENT

BY **Sid Goldstein**
Author of *The Wine Lover's Cookbook*

PHOTOGRAPHS BY **Paul Moore**

CHRONICLE BOOKS
SAN FRANCISCO

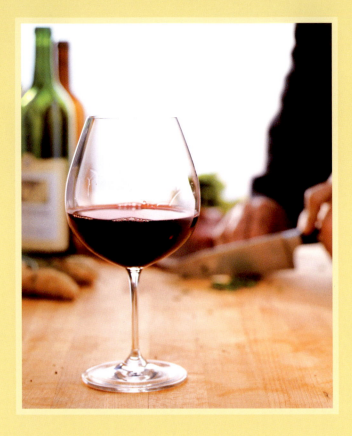

Text copyright © 2004 by Sid Goldstein.

Photographs copyright © 2004 by Paul Moore.

All rights reserved. No part of this book
may be reproduced in any form without written
permission from the publisher.

Library of Congress Cataloging-in-Publication Data:

Goldstein, Sid.
   The wine lover cooks with wine:great recipes
for the essential ingredient/by Sid Goldstein;
photographs by Paul Moore.
      p. cm.
   Includes bibliographical references and index.
   ISBN 0-8118-3022-5 (pbk.)
   1. Cookery (Wine) I. Title.
   TX726.G54 2004
   641.6'22—dc22

                                    2004005724

COVER: Seared Peppercorn and Spice–Crusted
Rib-Eye with Roquefort and Walnuts,
page 59

PAGE 2: Grilled Quail in Red Onion Escabeche,
page 125

Manufactured in Singapore.

Photography assistance by Jeff McLain

Prop Styling by George Dolese

Food Styling by Jason Wheeler

Design and typesetting by Betty Ho

The photographer would like to thank
Jeff McLain who assisted and managed
the photo workflow, George Dolese for his
keen eye for style, and Jason Wheeler for
helping out on food prep.

Distributed in Canada
by Raincoast Books
9050 Shaughnessy Street
Vancouver, British Columbia V6P 6E5

10 9 8 7 6 5 4 3

Chronicle Books LLC
85 Second Street
San Francisco, California 94105

www.chroniclebooks.com

Sid has always had a passion for the topic of food
and wine . . . cooking, consuming, and especially
writing about it. It was not long after *The Wine
Lover's Cookbook* was published that the concept for
The Wine Lover Cooks with Wine was conceived. In
July of 2001, shortly after submitting the first com-
pleted draft of his manuscript to Chronicle Books,
Sid suffered a near fatal cardiac arrest that left him
with a brain injury from which he continues to
recover. It was more than a year before he was able
to continue work on the book, incorporating the
edits necessary to bring the project to completion.
This process was very difficult, but at the same time
therapeutic for Sid, and he worked tirelessly to see
his book into publication.

I would like to thank Bill LeBlond, Amy Treadwell,
and all of the editorial staff at Chronicle Books for
their patience and faith in Sid and this project. I
would also like to express the love and admiration
I have for my husband and his courage to work
through his disability to achieve his goal. May you
enjoy cooking these recipes as much as he has
enjoyed bringing them to you!

                                    —SUZANNE GOLDSTEIN

CONTENTS

Acknowledgments

Having made it through my fifth and most challenging cookbook, I have many people to thank for their various consulting, culinary, and literary contributions. My thanks to:

All of the chefs who so graciously shared their recipes, for believing in the project. I learned so much from knowing you and talking to you that this book would truly not have been possible without you.

Bill LeBlond, editor extraordinaire at Chronicle Books, whose continued enthusiasm and faith in my work is a great motivator. And to the crackerjack editing, design, and production teams Amy Treadwell, Jan Hughes, Doug Ogan, Carolyn Miller, Brett MacFadden, and Beth Steiner, whose combined talent is what makes any author's book come to life.

My fearless and enthusiastic testers and readers, whose feedback is so critical: Dorothy Woll, Sandy Rogers, Lori Wood, Vici Resner, Meg McCarthy, Tim Sweeney, Don Miller, Hoke Harden, and Karen Boudrie.

John Ash, for his constant culinary inspiration and vision, and for his insightful recommendations early on in this project.

To my wonderful mother, Lois Jamart, who got me started on this path without my even knowing it. Thanks for feeding and loving me, Mom, and for your recipe testing and continued passion for food. And to Gus for being her wonderful, patient husband—with a great appetite at ninety-four young years.

Zack, my terrific, talented son and best buddy, whose palate keeps me grounded and who lights up my life. I'm glad you liked these recipes so much. I hope the cooking in college is as satisfying.

To Ruby, golden retriever of the most divine sort. Your unfailing desire to gobble any leftover food is a constant amazement, as is your smiling face and exuberant wagging afterwards, which I take as meaning "yummy, Dad."

And my wonderful wife of twenty-two years, Suzanne, for being my unwavering food and wine codependent as well as my true companion and loving soul mate. Thanks, too, for your fabulous desserts, which assure you of my constant admiration and devotion.

Thank you, thank you.

—SID GOLDSTEIN

Introduction

Since the time wine was first created in 5000 B.C., humans have found that its magical properties include not only its ability to delight the taste buds and to pleasantly intoxicate, but to help flavor and cook food, although the predominant use of wine in cooking came much later. In fact, wine's ability to infuse food with flavor is so multidimensional that it influences every method in which we cook and is at the heart of most of the world's great cuisines.

Wine tenderizes and adds moisture to food, as well as imparting a deep, complex flavor. No other single ingredient—not salt, spices, stock, or fat—has quite the same power to affect our cooking as wine does. And, in that very sense, wine is truly a "magical ingredient."

Whether wine is used to steam mussels, poach fresh fish, marinate and tenderize chicken or meat, add flavor to soups or stews, deglaze a roasting pan, or make desserts and drinks, it is a chameleon—capable of creating both delicacy and intensity in food.

Wine can add body, acidity, tartness, and sweetness as it joins with herbs, spices, and other ingredients to help transform and coax taste from our food. An old adage of the wine industry is that "wine is food." The cooking process underscores this point.

From Homer, we learn that early Greek and Roman civilizations embraced wine for cooking, and wine became well integrated into Mediterranean cuisine after large-scale plantings by the Romans. By the eighteenth century, dishes such as marinated lamb, pears in port, sherry-flavored puddings, and beef with claret were quickly becoming the hallmarks of cuisine.

In 1963, *Favorite Recipes of California Winemakers*, probably the first cookbook written about cooking with California wine, provided some insight: "Whoever first discovered the sudden flowering of flavor from pouring a little wine remains unknown, an unsung genius in gastronomical history. But legions of chefs and good home cooks would salute and bless his name if we knew it. It is a name lost in the fragrant vinous mists from millions of kitchens ever since, throughout the ages."

The Wine Lover Cooks with Wine explores the many ways in which wine is used in contemporary cooking. In my own kitchen, wine is prized not only for its ability to complement food at the table, but for the magical qualities that it contributes to the finished dish. In addition to some of my recipes, this book includes recipes and insight from some of America's best chefs. Most of the dishes are made with traditional and contemporary varietal wines, but Champagne, sherry, port, Madeira, Marsala, vermouth, sake, and mirin are also used. These unique wines are an important part of the liquid pantry.

Wine writer Matt Kramer has pointed out that "conviction is the motivator of compelling wine," illustrating that the steadfast commitment of a wine maker to grapes from a specific place begins to define a wine's uniqueness, if not greatness. If this is true—which it surely is—then cooking with wine also reflects a certain conviction and vision on the part of the cook. Wine is the element that transforms great ingredients into delicious food.

Since wine is prized for its inimitable flavor as a drinking beverage, it might at first seem almost disrespectful to cook with it, since the cooking process changes its very character, but that is exactly why cooks use wine. As wine cooks, the alcohol burns off, and the flavor of the wine adds complexity to our food. Uncooked wine is also used by many chefs to finish sauces and contribute a lively top note to a dish.

Recent studies by the Mayo Clinic show that anywhere from 15 to 95 percent of the alcohol in wine evaporates, depending on the cooking method utilized and the amount of time the wine cooks. According to this study, it takes 15 minutes for wine added to a boiling liquid to lose 60 percent of its alcohol, and nearly $2^1/2$ hours of cooking for wine to lose 95 percent of its alcohol, which is somewhat longer than conventional understanding. It's worth noting that as alcohol evaporates, so does about 85 percent of its calories.

When the alcohol burns off in wine, what's left is the essence of the wine itself, which includes its fruit and acidity. This brings us to Cooking with Wine Truth No. 1: Never use an inferior wine for cooking. The wine need not be the same wine that will be consumed with the dish; however, good-quality wines should always be used for cooking. A great sauce is never made with a poor wine.

A product labeled "cooking wine" often contains salt, herbs, spices, and food coloring. Legend has it that these wines were used in the eighteenth and nineteenth centuries to keep cooks in aristocratic kitchens from drinking the wine. They are hideous tasting; save yourself the misery. As a footnote, bottles listed as "cooking wine" often offer the disclaimer that the contents shouldn't be considered a beverage.

Because of the many varietals and styles of wine, its usage in cooking varies dramatically, from lusty meat dishes like Bradley Ogden's Braised Short Ribs with Leeks and Green Peas (page 178) to delicate desserts like Joyce Goldstein's Peach and Champagne Sorbet (page 208).

Some top chefs don't use wine in their cooking at all, as they feel it obscures the basic flavor of a dish. Wine's acidity, essential to certain sauces, can be intrusive in other dishes. Wine is not found in most Latin American–based recipes since it's not traditionally part of that culture. On the other hand, in classic French and traditional Italian cooking, as well as in contemporary American cuisine, which draws from both of these disciplines, wine is used prominently in many recipes. In Asian cooking, sake, mirin, and Shaoxing wine find their way into recipes because they are indigenous to Japanese and Chinese cultures.

Wine affects the flavor of food, whether it's utilized in an intense reduction sauce, a delicate steam, a rolling simmer, or an enveloping marinade. The role of wine in each of these techniques is different, from the featured attraction to a subtle support player.

The Wine Lover Cooks with Wine focuses on the cooking techniques that use wine rather than organizing recipes by courses. It is not the intent of this book to promote including wine in every dish, however subtle some of the uses might be, but to be an inspiring source of wine-based recipes.

The recipes in this book are divided into seven chapters: Sauces, Steaming, Simmering and Poaching, Marinating, Braising, non-wine-based Side Dishes that complement many entrées, and Desserts and Drinks.

In some cases, the decision on where to place a recipe was complicated when wine was used in multiple roles, such as in a marinade and then in a finished sauce. These recipes were grouped in the chapter in which the featured technique was most important in the finished dish. The Simmering and Poaching chapter thus includes those recipes in which wine is reduced to an essence, or is used to poach the food in the dish. Risotto fits into this chapter as well.

Wine, with its complex combination of three of the four basic tastes—sweet, sour, and bitter—and its generous offering of flavors is truly a "magical ingredient," and can be either simple or sublime. I can't imagine my kitchen or my table without it.

Varietal, Fortified, and Specialty Wines

Countless dishes from around the world would have a very different look, smell, and taste without the addition of wine. Food would be tougher and drier, and would not resonate with the depth of flavor that wine and its various derivatives give it.

This chapter explores the stylistic character of most of the prominent varietal table wines used in cooking. Additionally, fortified wines, such as sherry, port, Madeira, and Marsala, and specialty wines, such as Champagne, sake, mirin, Shaoxing wine (Chinese rice wine), retsina, and vermouth, will be briefly explored.

Light, Fruity Whites
Riesling
Gewürztraminer
Muscat
Chenin Blanc
Sauvignon/Fumé Blanc
Pinot Gris/Pinot Grigio
Trebbiano and Garganega
Pinot Blanc

Medium- to Full-Bodied Whites
Chardonnay
Viognier
Marsanne
Roussanne
Albariño

Light- to Medium-Bodied Reds
Gamay
Tempranillo
Pinot Noir
Sangiovese

Medium- to Full-Bodied Reds
Zinfandel
Merlot
Cabernet Sauvignon
Nebbiolo
Syrah/Shiraz

Fortified Wines
Sherry
Vermouth
Marsala
Madeira
Port

Specialty Wines
Champagne and sparkling wines
Sake, Mirin, and Shaoxing wine
Retsina
Verjus

LIGHT, FRUITY WHITES

Light, fruity white wines play an important role in cooking. These wines are typically fermented in stainless-steel tanks rather than oak barrels. Stylistically, they showcase a forward fruit character (which varies depending on the varietal), appealing freshness, and lively acidity.

Good acidity in wine provides a solid backbone for many kinds of sauces, helping to neutralize protein and fat. The fruit emphasis of these wines, ranging from citrus, apple, and pear to stone fruits such as apricot and peach, also makes a contribution to sauces by layering flavors and providing some aromatic profile, although a wine's aroma tends to decrease dramatically when it is cooked.

Riesling, Gewürztraminer, Muscat, and Chenin Blanc come in a wide array of styles, from bone dry to intensely sweet. Depending on the type of sauce desired and the other flavors and ingredients used in the sauce, these off-dry (or slightly sweet) to sweet wines can be an important part of the dish. Muscat, or Moscato as it's called in Italy, is a particularly intriguing wine with a musky, floral aroma and a relatively light body. It helps to flavor desserts such as Dried Apricot and Muscat Cheesecake in a Gingersnap Crust (page 206).

In one of the more adventuresome recipes in this book, Smoked Sea Scallops in Riesling "Martinis" (page 153), Riesling lends a fresh, fruity top note to balance the smoky flavor of the scallops; it adds a gentle accent to Caramelized Onion and Jalapeño Waffles with Smoked Salmon, Radish Salad, and Lemon Cream (page 82), one of the most interesting appetizers in the book.

Fruity, unoaked wines are particularly useful when combined with chilies or aromatic spices. Thai, Asian, and some Mediterranean dishes benefit from fruity and sometimes slightly sweet wines. Steaming with these wines releases a lovely perfume that leaves an indelible mark on some dishes, such as Steamed Mussels with Thai Curry Sauce (page 66).

Of all white wines, Sauvignon/Fumé Blanc probably offers the wine-loving cook the most versatility. With good intensity of flavor and excellent acidity, Sauvignon Blanc dazzles with its ability to infuse dishes with flavor, while providing the acidic underpinning that they need to stay "alive" on the palate.

Pinot Gris and its Italian counterpart Pinot Grigio offer a similarly crisp, fruity character with good acidity, although they lack some of the body and depth of flavor found in most Sauvignons/Fumé Blancs.

Trebbiano, the prolific white grape of Italy, produces the majority of light Italian whites such as Frascati and Orvieto and is a blending grape throughout Italy, while Garganega is the primary grape for Soave's offerings. Light, fruity, and delicate, it is an excellent wine for cooking, particularly with risotto.

Chenin Blanc, which has decreased tremendously in popularity over the past twenty years in California, is now a fairly inconsequential wine, except in the best growing areas. The Chenin Blanc from the Loire Valley in France is usually of high enough quality that it is more of a table wine than a cooking wine.

Pinot Blancs, particularly those from Alsace in France, are fine drinking wines, and are only occasionally used in cooking, except sparingly at the end of a sauce preparation.

MEDIUM- TO FULL-BODIED WHITES

Medium- to full-bodied whites have a definite role in cooking, although a slightly different one than lighter fruity wines. In braised dishes, particularly of veal, pork, or poultry, it's often desirable to use a more full-bodied wine to provide some heft and depth to the braising liquid. As protein commingles with these wines, a richer liquid and subsequent sauce results.

In these types of dishes, the oak that is present in most Chardonnays is less noticeable and actually adds an element of complexity to the sauce. Chardonnay's full, ripe fruit and often buttery texture, the results of its fermentation process and barrel-aging regime, add dimension to some sauces, particularly to white wine–butter sauces. The widespread availability of good Chardonnay at reasonable prices also makes it a popular cooking wine. When pairing wine with the finished dish, serving an even higher-quality Chardonnay at the table can produce a memorable match.

Aromatic medium- to full-bodied wines, like Viognier, Marsanne, Roussanne, and Albariño, have an enviable combination of good body, vibrant fruit, and moderate acidity, but the price of these wines prevents them from being used as cooking wines in most cases.

Albariño, a less-known varietal from the Rías Baixas region in Spain, is a medium- to full-bodied wine that is beginning to make a surge in the United States. Its aromatic floral bouquet and stone-fruit flavor make it a wine for the liquid pantry, although price might prevent its usage there.

LIGHT- TO MEDIUM-BODIED REDS

Lighter red wines, such as Gamay, Tempranillo, and lighter styles of both California Pinot Noir and Sangiovese, have some distinctive attributes when used for cooking. They are blessed—first off—by being red. A combination of brightness from good acidity, gentle fruit, and in some cases, a depth of flavor without jarring tannins makes them ideal for more elegant sauces.

While Pinot Noir is one of the greatest grapes in the world when grown in premier vineyards in Burgundy in France; in the Carneros, Russian River, and Santa Barbara regions of California; in parts of Australia and New Zealand; and in Oregon, less-expensive versions are more suitable to use in a sauce. In this book, Pinot Noir is featured in a delicious Coq au Vin (page 122), where it is simmered into an intense reduction. Its beguiling character is also captured in a unique dessert, Spiced Berry "Martinis" with Pinot Noir Syrup and Star Anise Ice Cream (page 199).

swagger, with an occasional layering of spice and pepper, helps to infuse meats with just the right touch of flavor intensity and body. The quintessentially American varietal also works well with grilled foods. It is slightly macho and compellingly brash.

Merlot and Cabernet Sauvignon, two of the world's great varietals, come in a wide range of price, quality, and intensity. While $75 Cabernet from Napa is not likely to become the basis for a sauce, decent-quality $8 to $10 Cabernet and Merlot can be found, and they are exceptionally good choices for that use. In dishes such as Merlot-Braised Peasant Chicken with Rigatoni (page 166), a good-quality wine makes a huge difference.

Fruit intensity, tannic backbone, and full body are hallmarks of these two varietals. Merlot tends to be a little softer and fruitier than Cabernet and is also less expensive. Both are tremendously popular for cooking and marry well with meat dishes.

Nebbiolo is a lesser-known varietal that is used to produce the great wines of the Piedmont region of northwestern Italy, home of Barolo and Barbaresco. Many classic Italian pastas and game dishes rely on the reduction of this very dark, intense wine, which is quite tannic when it's young. If a robust quality is desired, Nebbiolo (typically labeled Barolo and Barbaresco) is the ticket.

Syrah, and its Australian counterpart Shiraz, is another superb wine for cooking. Though this wine bridges an enormous price range, good-quality, inexpensive Syrah/Shiraz is widely available. As a cooking wine, its full body (resulting from fairly high alcohol), very ripe fruit with hints of chocolate and pepper, and intense

Sangiovese, the premier varietal of Tuscany in Italy, has been used in the hearty Italian cooking of the region for centuries. Its combination of bright cherry- and berry-tinged fruit combined with a generous amount of acidity, particularly when young, provides a vibrant base for rustic sauces, and it marries seamlessly with the acidity in tomatoes. Sangiovese plays a starring role here in Grilled Veal Chops with Pancetta and Porcini in Chianti Sauce (page 154), infusing the dish with liveliness.

Gamay has an almost white wine–like fruitiness and makes a lovely light pan sauce for chicken or seafood, while Tempranillo from the Rioja region of northern Spain offers a little more verve and depth for sauces with greater intensity. Relatively inexpensive, good-quality wines from all these varietals are worth using.

MEDIUM- TO FULL-BODIED REDS

Zinfandel may be the most perfect wine for marinating. Its combination of ripe fruit and youthful flavors can make beautiful, dark sauces that unveil deep flavor. The same can be said for Petite Sirah, a different varietal from Syrah/Shiraz, which offers deep fruit concentration and intensity. Hot Mulled "Touchdown" Shiraz (page 209) is a flavorful, robust warm drink that will delight your friends.

FORTIFIED WINES

Fortified wines (made with grape brandy added to a base wine after it has fermented, to increase body and alcohol) have a long and legendary place in the culinary pantheon. Whether used in desserts or as aromatic, complex additions to sauce and marinades, fortified wines offer full body (due to their higher alcohol), sweetness, and considerable intensity.

SHERRY

Sherries, of course, are mostly served as aperitif or dessert wines. They have an unusual nutty flavor and a somewhat exotic bouquet, making them the classic beverage to pair with tapas.

The great sherries from the Jerez region of southern Spain near Seville, made principally from the Palomino grape, are classically flavored with pear, roasted almonds and walnuts, dried fruit, and orange peel overtones. Whether a bone-dry Fino or Manzanilla; a slightly sweet Amontillado; an aromatic, dark, rich Oloroso; or a very sweet, viscous cream sherry made from the intense Pedro Ximénez grape, sherry has a more complex character than table wine.

Used judiciously, dry sherry adds a note of complexity that can help transform dishes such as Portuguese Steamed Clams with Sausage (page 70)

into something special. Sherry offers a bit more complexity than traditional table wines, but it should be used in dishes that are regionally appropriate, or where a hint of nuttiness is desirable.

VERMOUTH

Vermouth, other than "spoiling" many a martini aficionado's favorite drink, plays a decreasing role in contemporary cooking. Popular in the sixties and seventies, vermouth has lost some its fan base for no particular reason; it is a remarkably complex and interesting beverage with herb and spice overtones.

Vermouth is available both white and red and dry and sweet. Dry white vermouth is the most common. Named from the German word *wermut*, or "wormwood" (a bitter herb used in its flavoring), dry white vermouth has a bitter taste—its characteristic contribution to the martini—that can add a balancing note to a sauce. When added to a fish fumet, as in Vermouth-Poached Sea Bass with Orange-Jicama Salsa and Fried Capers (page 113), a lovely poaching liquid results.

Contemporary vermouth is made with relatively ordinary wines that are infused with aromatic roots; spices such as cloves, nutmeg, and orange peel; and a wide range of other barks, herbs, and flowers. In California, there has been a recent move by some producers to make higher-quality vermouth from French Colombard and Orange Muscat.

MARSALA

From western Sicily, Marsala is a sweet fortified wine made in oak barrels by a blending process similar to the solera method used for making sherry. Marsala is available either dry or sweet (*secco* or *dolce)* and varies greatly in quality, depending on the length of aging.

In the kitchen, Marsala's major claim to fame is in the Italian classic *zabaglione,* and it's prized in other Italian pastry desserts, often in combination with marzipan, due to its relatively powerful flavor.

MADEIRA

Madeira comes from the Portuguese island of the same name. Produced from the Malvasia grape, Madeira's fame is largely due to its reputation in England and the British colonies, where it has been revered for centuries and favored by kings and statesmen. The favorite drink of George Washington, and one of Thomas Jefferson's favored beverages, Madeira also has a place in American lore.

Madeira's caramelized, oxidative character is developed by fortifying it with grape spirits prior to the completion of fermentation, which is why it exhibits a characteristic sweetness. This was done in the early days to help it withstand long sea voyages to the East Indies. Madeira's unique flavors are a result of exposure to heat, originally from long days of sailing across the Equator, and today from being baked in hothouses lined with hot-water pipes or aged in large oak barrels in heated buildings.

Higher-quality dry Madeira is made from high-acid Sercial and Verdelho, and is favored by many chefs, although these Madeiras can be somewhat expensive. Sweeter versions of both of these wines are made through the addition of grape brandy; the bottles are stacked in attics rather than being baked for the maturation process.

Both Madeira and sherry have been traditionally added to hot consommé to give it a nutty, caramelized character. Sweeter Madeira, known as Bual or Malmsey, depending on the level of sweetness, is incredibly rich and viscous and is stunning with dried fruits and caramel- or toffee- or coffee-flavored desserts. Many enthusiasts feel that Madeira is best as a dessert on its own, or served after dessert.

Madeira's full, lush body and tangy acidity make it a very specialized cooking wine. It is used by some chefs in cream-based sauces.

PORT

Port enjoys an even greater reputation than Madeira in cooking. Early in the eighteenth century, port as we know it was born by adding 3 percent–alcohol clear grape spirits to relatively poor-quality, still-fermenting Portuguese wine, which yielded a wonderful elixir with a caramel-like sweet flavor.

Ranging from lighter tawny and ruby ports through serious, deeply flavored vintage bottlings, port comes in a diverse array of styles for both sipping and cooking needs. However, it would be rare to use a vintage port in cooking. Most successful results come from using a good-quality tawny or ruby port with a reasonably full body and good flavor.

Port—like Madeira—is often favored for sipping on its own; however, it enjoys an illustrious history as an ingredient in classic red wine sauces and as a poaching liquid for apples, pears, and other fruits. Often used to intensify the flavor of a red wine reduction, port adds an inimitable flavor to the sauce. Sauces that are too acidic can also be balanced with the addition of port or Madeira to help attenuate the tartness.

The sweet wine should be reduced first so that the alcohol burns off. If the sauce tastes too sweet, it can be balanced with a little balsamic or wine vinegar. One minor caveat with a port-reduced sauce is to ensure that it doesn't over-reduce and become too intense. It's also important that the sweetness of the sauce does not become greater than the red wine that will (presumably) be consumed with the dish, or it will make the wine taste drier and more acidic than it is.

With desserts, port is legendary. Port-Poached Pears with Cloves, Cinnamon, and Vanilla (page 200) is a good example of a port-infused dessert that integrates vanilla and spices. Chocolate- and coffee-based desserts can often be enlivened by the judicious use of port. While this is clearly a case of intensity meets intensity, few would argue with Emily Luchetti's fabulous Drunken Chocolate Cake with Port (page 196), as decadent and downright good as dessert is likely to get.

SPECIALTY WINES

CHAMPAGNE AND SPARKLING WINES
Champagne (and Champagne-style sparkling wines) as a culinary beverage has some specialized uses that make it justifiably important. Due to its effervescence and vibrant fruity character, it can be used for anything from sauces to desserts, sometimes with the alcohol boiled off and sometimes just splashed in for good measure.

There is one school of thought, however, that suggests that the use of Champagne in cooking is senseless due to the fact that a long reduction diminishes most of the subtlety and finesse of a better-quality Champagne and that a higher-acid white wine is just as suitable.

Champagne enjoys relatively low alcohol to begin with since the grapes are picked at lower levels of ripeness. Stylistic variations occur depending on the amount of dosage (sugar) added. These styles are generally referred to as *brut* (less than 1.5 percent sugar), *sec* (from 1.5 percent to 3 percent sugar), *demi-sec* (from 3 percent to 6 percent and discernibly sweet), and *cremant* (lightly sparkling and sweet).

Only Champagnes made in the Champagne region of France are allowed to carry that name; all other wines, even if made by the Champagne method, must be referred to simply as *sparkling wines*. Other sparkling wines are the soft and lightly sweet Italian prosecco and Asti, a floral-imbued sparkler made from Moscato Canelli. Both are very pleasant poured over fresh berries and other fruits.

Chef Phil McGauley's Prosciutto and Walnut–Stuffed Chicken Breasts with Roasted Red Pepper and Champagne Cream (page 42) utilizes Champagne to enliven a fairly rich roasted pepper–infused cream sauce. The Champagne pulls the whole dish together and provides balance.

SAKE, MIRIN, AND SHAOXING WINE
Rice was first cultivated in Japan over two thousand years ago, but it took some time to develop sake, the classic fermented and brewed beverage of

Japan, which transforms rice grains into something incomparable and sublime. In fact, sake's true origins are in Korea and China, where it first appeared in the second century A.D. Consumed at many ceremonies and rituals involving large groups, sake also has a role in the contemporary kitchen, where its fruity flavor, tangy acidity, and relatively high alcohol make an imprint on many an Asian dish. Sake is particularly prized in seafood dishes, such as Clams Steamed in Lemongrass and Ginger–Infused Sake (page 71), where its aromatic, fruitlike character helps to transform the ingredients.

Mirin is a sweet, almost syrupy rice-based cooking wine that sometimes has a little salt added; it nicely counterbalances soy-based marinades, dipping sauces, and broths, as in Steamed Shiitake and Spinach Wontons in Mirin Broth (page 73).

Shaoxing wine, a Chinese rice wine made from rice, Jian Lake water, and a yeast allegedly in use for two thousand years, is a unique cooking wine. Sometimes called "yellow wine," Shaoxing is fairly high in alcohol (17 percent is not uncommon). It finds its way into an adaptation of Barbara Tropp's Green Onion and Ginger Explosion Shrimp (page 115). If Shaoxing is not available, a dry sherry is the most suitable substitute.

Sake comes in such a wide range of styles—from dry to sweet, clear to cloudy, delicate to full, young to aged—that it's impossible to be too specific about which one to use in cooking. The key to using sake is to keep it fresh. Store it in a cool, dark place, like a wine cellar or refrigerator, and consume it within a year.

RETSINA

This Greek wine originated when the ceramic amphorae in which the wine was stored were sealed with pine resin. The resin slowly leeched into the wine, and a taste for pine resin–infused wines developed. Later, infusion of pine resin during fermentation became commonplace. Better retsinas are now made from the Savatiano grape.

Retsina's controversial turpentine flavor does not reap rhapsodic acclaim, but this wine has a place in Greek cooking. It is a suitable contrast to salty olives and feta cheese, as in Greek-Style Shrimp with Retsina and Feta (page 121). A little retsina goes a long way, but it's an interesting flavoring.

VERJUS

Verjus is not a wine at all, but it's included here because it is the predecessor of wine: unfermented grape juice. Literally meaning "green juice," verjus originated in France and is now being popularized in California and Long Island. It has a crisp, spunky, nonalcoholic taste that can often replace vinegar in recipes, making it easier to pair the finished dishes with wine.

Poaching in verjus is a common utilization. Many chefs also favor verjus instead of wine in stocks and demi-glaces, finding that its green-grape character brings out the flavor of meat-focused dishes. In this book, verjus "marinates" a fish dish: a Caper and Olive–Encrusted Petrale Sole with Verjus and Lemon (page 146). Use this worthwhile addition when wine would be too powerful or intrusive, or when the wine could not be adequately cooked off.

10 TIPS ON COOKING WITH WINE

1   Never use inferior-quality wine in your cooking. While the wine used for cooking does not have to be expensive, it should be of good commercial quality. When the alcohol evaporates, what's left is the *flavor* of the wine.

2   Use fresh wines when cooking. Older wines that have been left for more than 2 weeks in the refrigerator will have oxidized somewhat and will not complement your cooking.

3   A good rule of thumb is to use red wines with red meats, game, and duck, and white wines with pork, veal, poultry, and seafood. With spicy or fruity dishes, dry, unoaked whites or off-dry, slightly sweet wines, such as Riesling and Gewürztraminer, can add bright fruit and acidity to the dish.

4   If a white wine reduction is too tart, a little salt in the sauce can balance it, whereas the addition of a little sugar or honey will adjust a red wine reduction.

5   The least intrusive, most delicate cooking method with wine is steaming; here, the wine is used for its aromatic contribution and wet heat and is not in direct contact with the food.

6   Braising meats and vegetables slowly in wine for a long period of time allows the wine to tenderize the meat and infuses the dish with an incomparable flavor.

7   Be careful not to over-reduce sauces. The thicker the reduction, the more intense the sauce, which may not always be what's desired. If necessary, add a splash of wine to a finished reduction to soften its effect slightly.

8   Using wines in marinades is very effective, as it allows the wine to slightly tenderize the meat and acts as a "carrier," helping the meat to absorb the flavors of aromatic vegetables, herbs, and seasonings. Tender cuts need far less time in a marinade than tougher cuts.

9   Use sweet wines, such as port, Madeira, Marsala, sweet sherry, vermouth, and mirin more sparingly than dry wines, as they can easily overpower a dish.

10 The old cook's adage is "A jigger to drink with every jigger that's used in the dish." But remember to get the dish cooked properly before the guests arrive!

Sauces

It seems somewhat presumptuous to take on the challenge of writing a chapter about sauces since entire volumes have been written on them. Nevertheless, a book about cooking with wine should explore sauces in some depth since they are so essential to the subject.

The origin of sauces more than likely came about in the first century A.D., in *De condituris,* a cookbook written by Apicius. Known as "juices," they were heavily spiced and thickened with bread. Typical ingredients included fermented fish paste, wine, onions, pine nuts, pepper, and oil.

In Auguste Escoffier's *Guide Culinaire,* published in 1902, no fewer than two hundred sauces are listed, although his primary contribution was to classify sauces into five "mother sauces" —béchamel, espagnole, hollandaise, tomato, and velouté. Wine is a consequential part of classic espagnole, or brown, sauces, such as bordelaise, diable, lyonnaise, Madeira, Perigueux, piquante, Robert, chasseur, and red wine reductions. In France, where sauce is king, one classic is called *marchand de vin,* or "wine merchant's sauce."

Wine is also a key component in white bordelaise, ravigote, béarnaise, beurre blanc, and beurre rouge sauces. Wine in sauces can be either the star ingredient or the support player, but it's almost always a "magical ingredient," bringing qualities to the sauce that are not otherwise attainable.

Mastering the Art of French Cooking by Julia Child, Louisette Bertholle, and Simone Beck, defines *sauté* as: "To cook and brown food in a very small quantity of very hot fat, usually in an open skillet." One of the primary reasons for sautéing meats and vegetables is to brown them and to seal in their juices. This allows for a subsequent deglazing with wine, which, in some cases, is followed by a reduction sauce.

Wine is the liquid of choice for deglazing, a relatively simple technique. Prior to adding the wine, the seared meat is removed and the fat is poured off, then the wine is added and the mixture is stirred while the browned bits on the bottom of the pan are scraped up. The result is a pan sauce with an acidic, fruity flavor.

When wine is used to deglaze, most of the alcohol burns off in a couple of minutes, whereas when used in sauces with stock and other ingredients, thirty minutes to an hour might be required to evaporate all of the alcohol. This relates in part to the heat of the pan at the time the wine is splashed into it.

Most sauces call for reducing the volume of wine by at least half before proceeding with the addition of stock and other ingredients to finish a sauce. This is accomplished by boiling or simmering the wine until the alcohol is burned off entirely.

In a classic white or red wine butter sauce (beurre blanc or beurre rouge), wine and vinegar are simmered and reduced with minced shallots. Cold butter is then beaten into the reduction to make a thick rich sauce.

Another kind of reduction sauce begins with a sauté of shallots, onions, or garlic with mushrooms and other aromatic vegetables. The vegetables are "sweated" (cooked in a covered heavy pan until they reduce liquid but do not color), then wine is added and reduced. The sauce then goes through a secondary reduction with stock. This technique is used in many of the recipes in this book and is favored by many contemporary chefs. Good-quality stock is highly desirable when making these sauces, although canned low-salt broth will suffice.

With butter- and cream-based sauces using wine, it's important that all the alcohol in the wine is burned off before adding the butter or cream, which is referred to as giving the sauce a liaison. Finished butter sauces must be served immediately, or kept warm over barely tepid water so that the emulsion formed between the fat in the butter and the cooking liquid doesn't "break," allowing free fat to float to the top of the sauce.

Wines behave somewhat differently in sauces, depending on how they're used. When a white wine is first reduced for a butter sauce, its concentrated acidity plays a pivotal role in creating the base for that sauce. On the other hand, when a red wine is combined with meat or fish, or is used in conjunction with a stock, the commingling of tannins in the wine with the protein in the food greatly reduces its tannic astringency. This process typically takes at least 30 minutes and is particularly important if butter is not used to ameliorate the astringency in the finished sauce.

The general rule with sauces is to use about 1 part wine to 3 or 4 parts other liquid, such as stock, cream, or melted butter. Too much wine in the dish and its acidity and tannin can overpower the sauce. Yet, wine's magical properties also include glycerin, a key element that helps it to bind sauces.

In contemporary kitchens, including my own, the role of fat in finishing sauces has changed dramatically. Many chefs are choosing to serve reduced sauces with little or no addition of butter or cream, due to dietary reasons. I personally find wine-based sauces that have been reduced with stock to be delightfully flavorful and texturally pleasing without the addition of butter or cream.

While sauces with no butter added might not have the sheen or consistency of a sauce finished with butter, they are much cleaner and fresher tasting. The use of a demi-glace (a highly reduced stock with intense flavors and a great deal of protein) also helps bind sauces. Alternatively, cornstarch or arrowroot mixed with water can be used.

A common practice used by many top chefs is to splash in a bit of a good-quality wine at the end to brighten a sauce just before plating. This brings out a fresh, vibrant character that helps to balance and "awaken" the sauce.

Wine's role in cooking is to integrate flavors: to act as a conduit and create harmony and balance. Without it, sauces would be flat, one-dimensional, and lacking structure.

RECOMMENDED WINES FOR SAUCES

WINE	TYPE OF SAUCE
Sauvignon Blanc/Fumé Blanc	Butter sauces, herb-based sauces for vegetables
Muscadet	Butter sauces
Pinot Gris/Pinot Grigio	Butter sauces, seafood sauces
Chardonnay	Reduction sauces for seafood, veal, poultry
Riesling/Gewürztraminer	Delicate sauces, spicy sauces
Cabernet Sauvignon	Reduction sauces for meat and game
Merlot	Reduction sauces for meat and game
Syrah/Shiraz	Reduction sauces for meat and game
Zinfandel	Spicier reduction sauces
Pinot Noir	Delicate reductions, with meat, poultry, and seafood

SAUCES

TIPS ON USING WINE IN SAUCES

- One simple truth is consistent to all cooking methods: Always use a good-quality wine.

- Lighter, more delicate, lower-alcohol wines, such as Sauvignon/Fumé Blanc, Riesling, Pinot Grigio/Gris, Sangiovese, Tempranillo (Spanish Rioja), and Pinot Noir, are generally used in more delicate sauces.

- Chardonnay, Merlot, Cabernet Sauvignon, Zinfandel, and Syrah/Shiraz are favored in more intense sauces.

- For butter sauces, higher-acid wines, such as Muscadet (native to Brittany, where butter sauces originated), Sauvignon/Fumé Blanc, or Pinot Gris/Grigio, are preferred.

- Use low-salt stocks and broths in making sauces, since salt intensifies when it's reduced and can overpower the subtleties of a good sauce.

- Hold butter sauces in a covered pot on a warm spot on the stove or over barely tepid water. If they thicken too much, stock, water, or cream can be added to maintain proper consistency.

- If wine sauces are being finished with cream, it is important that the alcohol has first burned off, since the addition of cream can cause curdling.

- If a slightly thicker consistency is desired in a sauce without adding butter or cream, a mixture of 1 part cornstarch and 1 part cold water stirred into the sauce will work.

- Never use too much wine in a sauce or it will dominate the flavor. Wine's role is to balance, not to overpower.

Corn and Chive Crepes with Wild Mushrooms

Recommended wine:
Chardonnay

Alternative wine:
Pinot Noir

Whether served as a brunch dish, a dinner entrée, or a first course, these savory crepes with corn, mushrooms, and sun-dried tomatoes will please with their hearty flavors. This recipe is adapted from one by Diane Pariseau, whose Trilogy Restaurant in the Napa Valley in California set an early standard for wine-country cooking. Serve with a buttery Chardonnay or a lighter Pinot Noir.

3/4 cup dry-packed sun-dried tomato halves

CREPES

1 cup corn kernels (2 ears)

2 tablespoons chicken stock

1 egg, beaten

1 tablespoon minced fresh chives

1 tablespoon minced fresh oregano, or 1/2 tablespoon dried oregano

1/3 teaspoon salt

1/8 teaspoon cayenne pepper

1/3 cup all-purpose flour, plus more as needed

1/2 cup milk, plus more as needed

2 tablespoons unsalted butter, melted

Soak the sun-dried tomatoes in warm water to cover for 30 minutes. Drain and cut into slices.

TO MAKE THE CREPES: In a blender or food processor purée the corn kernels. Add the stock and process again. Strain the liquid into a medium bowl and discard the solids. Add the egg, chives, oregano, salt, and cayenne and mix together. Add the $1/3$ cup flour, $1/2$ cup milk, and melted butter. Whisk vigorously until smooth. Let rest for at least 1 hour. The mixture should be the consistency of heavy cream. Thin with more milk or thicken with extra flour, if necessary.

Preheat the oven to 250°F. Heat an 8-inch nonstick pan or crepe pan over medium-high heat. Whisk the batter and add 2 tablespoons to the pan, immediately tilting the pan so that batter coats the pan evenly. When the crepe is light brown on the bottom, use a spatula to turn it over and cook for a few seconds on the other side. Place on a baking sheet.

Repeat to use all the batter, placing each crepe between a layer of waxed paper on a baking sheet. Cover with a damp cloth and place in a low oven.

FILLING

4 tablespoons unsalted butter

8 ounces shiitake mushrooms, stemmed and sliced

6 ounces oyster mushrooms, sliced

2 tablespoons minced shallots

1 tablespoon chopped fresh oregano or 1/2 teaspoon dried oregano

1/2 cup dry white wine

1/2 cup chicken stock

1/3 cup heavy cream or half-and-half

Kosher salt and freshly ground pepper

Fresh oregano sprigs and corn kernels for garnish

TO MAKE THE FILLING: In a medium sauté pan, melt the butter over medium heat. Add the mushrooms and shallots and sauté until the mushrooms start to wilt, 5 to 6 minutes. Add the sun-dried tomatoes and oregano; sauté 2 to 3 minutes. Add the wine and stock and cook to reduce by one-half. Add the cream or half-and-half and cook to reduce until thick enough to coat a spoon. Remove from heat and season with salt and pepper.

To serve, lay 1 crepe on each of 6 warmed plates. Divide the filling among the crepes, placing it in a ribbon in the center of each crepe, and fold the crepe in half. Garnish with oregano sprigs and corn kernels. Serve at once.

~Makes 6 crepes; serves 6 as a first course~

Goat Cheese and Raisin–Stuffed Poblano Chilies
with Roasted-Garlic Sauce

Recommended wine:
Sauvignon/Fumé Blanc

Alternative wine:
Marsanne or Roussanne

This recipe, inspired by *Bradley Ogden's Breakfast, Lunch, and Dinner*, has evolved considerably in my kitchen. The white wine–based roasted-garlic sauce is a sublime partner for the stuffed chilies. The intense flavors are nicely contrasted by a fruity Sauvignon/Fumé Blanc or an unoaked Marsanne or Roussanne.

ROASTED-GARLIC SAUCE

2 heads garlic, roasted (see note)

3/4 cup dry white wine

3/4 cup low-salt chicken stock

2 shallots, thinly sliced

3/4 cup heavy cream or half-and-half

Kosher salt and freshly ground pepper

4 poblano or Anaheim chilies, roasted and peeled (see note)

2 tablespoons olive oil

1/4 cup pine nuts

1/4 teaspoon minced fresh thyme, or pinch of dried thyme

2/3 cup fresh white goat cheese at room temperature

3 tablespoons golden raisins

2 tablespoons minced fresh flat-leaf parsley

2 tablespoons minced fresh basil, or 1 tablespoon dried basil

Preheat the oven to 350°F.

TO MAKE THE SAUCE: In a small saucepan, combine the roasted garlic pulp, white wine, stock, and shallots. Bring to a simmer over medium heat. Cover the pan, reduce heat to low, and simmer for 10 to 15 minutes. Add the cream or half-and-half, bring to a slow boil over medium heat, and cook to reduce the sauce until it coats a spoon. Season with salt and pepper. Set aside.

Cut a small slit in the side of each chili and remove the seeds, leaving the stem intact.

In a small sauté pan or skillet, heat 1 tablespoon of the olive oil over low heat. Add the pine nuts and toast to a golden brown, tossing frequently so they don't burn. Stir in the thyme and empty the mixture into a bowl.

Put the goat cheese in a small bowl and stir until smooth. Stir in the pine nuts, raisins, herbs, and salt and pepper to taste. Stuff the chilies carefully with the cheese mixture. Fold over the opening. Place, seam-side up, on a lightly oiled baking sheet. Drizzle with the remaining 1 tablespoon olive oil.

Bake the chilies until just heated through, about 15 minutes. Reheat the garlic sauce and spoon onto warmed plates. Place a stuffed chili on each plate. Garnish with the greens and bell pepper.

Kosher salt and freshly ground pepper

Lightly dressed mixed greens and chopped red bell pepper for garnish

✣ NOTE: **To roast garlic,** cut off the whole heads one-fourth of the way from the top. Place in a small baking dish and drizzle with olive oil. Sprinkle with salt and pepper. Cover tightly with aluminum foil. Roast in a preheated 350°F oven until soft, about 1 hour. Squeeze the garlic from its husk.

✣ NOTE: **To roast and peel peppers and chilies,** char whole peppers and chilies over an open gas flame, over hot coals, or under a pre-heated broiler until the skin blisters. Place them in a plastic or paper bag and let cool to the touch. Peel off the skin and discard. Cut out the stem and remove the seeds. Avoid touching your eyes or nose while working with chilies. Wash your hands thoroughly in hot, soapy water when done.

~Serves 4 as a first course~

Asian Eggplant Salad

Recommended wine:
Sake

Alternative wine:
Riesling

Sake is not well known as a cooking wine to most Westerners, though it adds a slightly sweet, almost nutty, flavor that is quite pleasing in some dishes. This Asian-style eggplant dish resonates with a bit of heat, so sip a good chilled sake or fruity Riesling with it. Serve this as a tantalizing room-temperature appetizer or as a side dish to grilled fish, chicken, or steak.

7 Japanese eggplants, halved length-wise (about 1 pound)

1/3 teaspoon kosher salt

1/2 cup sake

1 1/2 tablespoons olive oil

2 tablespoons chili oil

1 yellow onion, thinly sliced

3 cloves garlic, minced

2 1/2 tablespoons minced fresh ginger

1 stalk lemongrass (white part only), peeled and chopped (optional)

1 tablespoon fresh lime juice

1 tablespoon seasoned rice vinegar

1 tablespoon oyster sauce

1 tablespoon packed brown sugar

3/4 tablespoon smooth peanut butter

3 to 4 tablespoons toasted pine nuts (see note)

Kosher salt

Red pepper flakes

2 teaspoons sesame seeds, lightly toasted, for garnish (see note, page 41)

Preheat the oven to 350°F. Put the eggplants on paper towels, cut-side up, and sprinkle with the salt. Let rest for 30 minutes. Rinse and pat dry with paper towels. Place on a baking sheet and roast until they begin to soften, 25 to 30 minutes. Remove from the oven, cut into cubes, and set aside.

Meanwhile put the sake in a small saucepan and simmer over low heat to reduce by half. Set aside.

In a large sauté pan or skillet, heat the olive and chili oils over medium-high heat. Add the onion, garlic, ginger, and lemongrass and sauté until the onion is translucent, 3 to 4 minutes. Add the reduced sake, lime juice, vinegar, and oyster sauce, and simmer for 3 to 4 minutes. Add the brown sugar, peanut butter, and pine nuts. Stir well and heat through. Stir in the eggplant. Remove from heat and let cool. Season with salt and red pepper flakes.

Serve at room temperature, garnished with sesame seeds.

✺ NOTE: **To toast nuts,** place on a baking sheet and bake in a pre-heated 400°F oven for 5 to 8 minutes until lightly browned. Season to taste, if desired.

~*Serves 4 as an appetizer or side dish*~

Curried Scallops with Grapefruit and Ginger–White Wine Butter Sauce

White wine butter sauce, or beurre blanc, is a mainstay of classic French cuisine. An emulsification of reduced white wine and butter, this version includes grapefruit juice and fresh ginger to counterpoint the curried scallops. A fruity Australian or California Riesling or a New Zealand Sauvignon Blanc is a crisp, refreshing companion.

Recommended wine:
Riesling

Alternative wine:
Sauvignon/Fumé Blanc

GINGER–WHITE WINE
BUTTER SAUCE

7 tablespoons cold unsalted butter, cut into tablespoon-sized pieces

1 tablespoon minced shallots

1 1/2 tablespoons minced fresh ginger

1/2 cup dry white wine

1/2 cup fresh pink grapefruit juice

1/2 cup low-salt fish stock or clam juice

16 sea scallops (about 1 3/4 pounds total)

1 teaspoon curry powder

Kosher salt and freshly ground pepper

3 tablespoons unsalted butter

GARNISH

8 ruby grapefruit wedges

1 tablespoon minced fresh chives, plus 8 whole chives

TO MAKE THE SAUCE: In a heavy saucepan, melt 1 tablespoon of the butter over medium-high heat. Add the shallots and ginger and sauté for 3 to 4 minutes. Add the wine and cook to reduce to a glaze. Add the grapefruit juice and stock and bring to a boil. Reduce heat to a simmer and cook to reduce by half. Strain and return to the same pan. Remove from heat and whisk the remaining 6 tablespoons butter into the sauce 1 tablespoon at a time. Keep warm over barely tepid water, or cover and set in a warm place.

In a large bowl, combine the scallops, curry powder, salt, and pepper. Toss to coat. In a large sauté pan or skillet, melt the 3 tablespoons butter over medium-high heat. Add the scallops and sauté, turning often, until seared on the outside and just barely opaque throughout, 3 to 4 minutes. Remove from heat.

To serve, drizzle the sauce evenly onto warmed plates. Put 4 scallops in the center of each plate. Place 2 grapefruit wedges to one side of each plate. Sprinkle with minced chives. Place 2 chives standing up among each serving of scallops.

~Serves 4 as a generous first course~

Chicken Caesar Scallops with Parmesan Crisps

Recommended wine:
Pinot Noir

Alternative wine:
Chardonnay

This is an adaptation of a recipe by Jimmy Boyce, chef at Mary Elaine's at the Phoenician in Scottsdale, Arizona. It's a twist on Caesar salad that incorporates many of the same ingredients, such as romaine, anchovies, garlic, and Parmesan. Pinot Noir is used to deglaze the pan, while Chardonnay is used to wilt the romaine.

4 chicken thighs, rinsed and skinned

Kosher salt and freshly ground pepper

4 tablespoons olive oil

8 garlic cloves

1/2 cup red wine, preferably Pinot Noir

1 1/2 cups low-salt chicken stock

2 heads romaine lettuce

2 tablespoons unsalted butter

One 1-inch piece fresh ginger, peeled and cut into quarters

1/2 cup dry white wine, preferably Chardonnay

1/2 cup water

PARMESAN CRISPS

1/3 cup (3 ounces) grated Parmesan cheese

Season the chicken thighs generously with salt and pepper. In a large sauté pan or skillet, heat 2 tablespoons of the oil over medium heat. Sear the chicken until well browned, 2 to 3 minutes on each side. Add the garlic and cook for 2 to 3 minutes. Reduce heat, add the red wine, and simmer to reduce by two-thirds. Add the stock and cook until the chicken is opaque throughout, about 12 minutes. Remove from heat, let cool slightly, and slice the meat from the bones. Set aside and keep warm. Cook the sauce to reduce until thickened. Set aside and keep warm.

Cut about 1 1/2 inches from the top of each head of romaine and trim 1 inch from the root end. Cut each romaine head in half, rinse, and dry thoroughly. Season lightly with salt and pepper.

In a very large sauté pan or skillet, melt the butter over medium-high heat. Add the romaine and ginger and sauté until lightly browned. Reduce heat, add the white wine, and cook until the wine is evaporated. Add the water and cook until the water is evaporated and the romaine is wilted, 10 to 12 minutes. Remove from heat. Discard the ginger and season to taste. Keep warm.

TO MAKE THE PARMESAN CRISPS: Preheat the broiler. Spread the Parmesan evenly in an ovenproof nonstick sauté pan or skillet. Place under the broiler until golden brown, 5 to 6 minutes. Remove the crisp from the pan with a spatula and let cool. Break or cut into 4 pieces for a garnish.

12 large sea scallops

8 anchovies, drained and patted dry
(optional)

8 small marinated artichoke hearts,
drained and halved

8 niçoise olives, pitted

In a large sauté pan or skillet, heat the remaining 2 tablespoons olive oil over medium heat. Season the scallops with salt and pepper and add to the pan, making sure they are not too close together. Cook the scallops until golden brown, 3 to 4 minutes on each side. Transfer to a plate and keep warm.

To serve, divide the chicken thigh meat into 8 portions and the romaine into 12 portions. Place 1 portion of romaine in the center of each warmed plate. Place 1 portion of chicken on top of the lettuce. Repeat with another portion of romaine and chicken. Finish with a layer of romaine. Pour the pan sauce around the stack. Place 3 scallops on top of the stack, then garnish the top with a Parmesan crisp and 2 anchovies, if desired. Place 2 pieces of artichoke and 2 olives around each stack.

~Serves 4 as an entrée~

Chicken Marsala

Recommended wine:
Viognier

Alternative wine:
Chardonnay

Chicken Marsala is as traditionally Italian as it gets. A fortified wine produced in Sicily, Marsala may be either dry or sweet. This recipe utilizes the sweet version, which adds a luscious, caramelized raisinlike note to the sauce. Serve this with buttered spinach and pasta. An aromatic Viognier or Chardonnay, with its own exotic perfume, harmonizes well with the dish.

2/3 cup all-purpose flour

3/4 teaspoon kosher salt, plus more to taste

3/4 teaspoon freshly ground pepper, plus more to taste

1 tablespoon dried marjoram or oregano

1 teaspoon fennel seed, toasted and ground (see note)

4 skinless, boneless chicken breast halves, rinsed and patted dry

2 1/2 tablespoons olive oil

4 ounces pancetta, chopped

8 ounces cremini or shiitake mushrooms, sliced (stem shiitakes)

2 cloves garlic, minced

1 large shallot, minced

1 2/3 cups sweet Marsala wine

3/4 cup low-salt chicken stock

1 tablespoon tomato paste

1 1/2 tablespoons balsamic vinegar

In a small bowl, combine the flour, 3/4 teaspoon salt, 3/4 teaspoon pepper, marjoram or oregano, and ground fennel. Stir to blend. Transfer to a pie plate. Coat both sides of the chicken breasts, shaking off the excess. Set aside on waxed paper.

In a large sauté pan or skillet, heat 2 tablespoons of the oil over high heat until the surface shimmers. Add the chicken and brown on one side for 4 to 5 minutes. Turn the chicken, using tongs, and cook on the second side until golden brown on the outside and opaque throughout, 3 to 4 minutes. Transfer to a plate, cover loosely with aluminum foil, and keep warm in a low oven until ready to serve.

Heat the same pan, over medium heat, and sauté the pancetta until crisp, 5 to 6 minutes. Using a slotted spoon, transfer to paper towels to drain.

Add the remaining 1/2 tablespoon olive oil to the pan and sauté the mushrooms until they begin to brown, 5 to 6 minutes. Add the garlic and shallot and cook for 2 minutes. Add the Marsala and stir to scrape up the browned bits from the bottom of the pan. Add the stock, tomato paste, and pancetta. Simmer to reduce the sauce until thickened. Add the balsamic vinegar and juices accumulated on the plate holding the chicken. Remove from heat and whisk in the butter 1 tablespoon at a time. Season with salt and pepper. Stir in the minced parsley.

4 tablespoons unsalted butter at room temperature

1/2 cup minced fresh flat-leaf parsley, plus sprigs for garnish

To serve, place each chicken breast on a plate and cover with sauce. Garnish with parsley sprigs and serve immediately.

❊ NOTE: **To toast seeds,** spread the seeds on a baking sheet and toast in a preheated 350°F oven for 7 to 8 minutes, or until lightly browned.

~Serves 4 as an entrée~

Prosciutto and Walnut–Stuffed Chicken Breasts with Roasted Red Pepper and Champagne Cream

Recommended wine:
Champagne/sparkling wine

Alternative wine:
Chardonnay

Created by Phil McGauley, executive chef at Korbel Champagne winery in Guerneville, California, this dish was designed to showcase the vibrant flavors of a good Champagne. The pairing works supremely well with a full-bodied wine, particularly one made predominantly from the Chardonnay grape.

3 tablespoons olive oil

1 large yellow onion, chopped

3 garlic cloves, minced

2 cups (8 ounces) grated dry Monterey Jack cheese

3/4 cup walnuts, toasted and coarsely chopped (see note, page 35)

2 tablespoons minced fresh sage, or 1/2 tablespoon ground dried sage

2 tablespoons minced fresh chives

1 tablespoon minced fresh flat-leaf parsley

Kosher salt and freshly ground pepper

8 boneless, skinless chicken breast halves

8 thin slices of prosciutto

In a medium sauté pan or skillet, heat 1 tablespoon olive oil over medium heat and sauté the onion and garlic until soft, 5 to 7 minutes. Transfer to a medium bowl. Stir in the cheese, walnuts, sage, chives, parsley, salt, and pepper. Set aside.

Place each chicken breast between 2 pieces of plastic wrap. Pound with a mallet until evenly 1/4 inch thick. Remove from the plastic wrap and lay each piece of chicken on a cutting board. Cover each chicken breast with 1 slice of prosciutto. Divide the onion mixture evenly over the prosciutto. Roll up each chicken breast jelly-roll style, securing it with toothpicks, and season with salt and pepper.

TO MAKE THE CREAM: In a medium saucepan, heat the 1 teaspoon olive oil over medium heat. Add the shallots and sauté until soft, about 3 minutes. Add the Champagne and cook to reduce to 1/4 cup. Add the cream or half-and-half and cook to reduce to about 1 cup. Strain and set aside.

In a blender or food processor, combine the roasted bell peppers, roasted garlic, roasted shallots, and vinegar. Purée until smooth. With the machine running, drizzle in the 1/4 cup olive oil. Season with salt and pepper. Set aside.

ROASTED RED PEPPER AND
CHAMPAGNE CREAM

1 teaspoon olive oil, plus 1/4 cup

1 tablespoon minced shallots

2 cups Champagne or other sparkling
wine

3 cups heavy cream or half-and-half

2 large red bell peppers, roasted,
peeled, and chopped (see note,
page 33)

2 roasted garlic bulbs (see note,
page 33)

2 shallots, roasted and peeled
(see note)

1 tablespoon balsamic or red wine
vinegar

Kosher salt and freshly ground
pepper

Preheat the oven to 400°F. In a large ovenproof sauté pan or skillet, heat the remaining 2 tablespoons olive oil over medium heat. Sauté the chicken, in batches if necessary, until golden brown on all sides. Remove the toothpicks. Transfer to the oven and bake until opaque throughout, 10 to 15 minutes.

To serve, cut each chicken roll into thin slices. Spoon the cream evenly onto warmed plates and top with the chicken slices. Drizzle the red pepper mixture over the chicken.

❈ NOTE: **To roast shallots,** wrap the shallots in aluminum foil and roast in a preheated 350°F oven for about 45 minutes, or until soft.

~Serves 8 as an entrée~

Spice-Rubbed Pork Chops with Leek-Chipotle Sauce

Recommended wine:
Syrah/Shiraz

Alternative wine:
Brut rosé Champagne

This tasty dish relies on the beguiling heat of the chili powder used in the spice rub, the chipotle chilies (smoked jalapeños) in the sauce, and the Anaheim chilies in the stuffing. A fruity red wine, such as a young Syrah/Shiraz or a brut rosé Champagne, will help to tame the beautiful wildness of the chilies. Serve this with sautéed spinach and dilled carrots.

6 thick-cut pork chops, trimmed of fat (about 2 1/2 pounds total)

SPICE RUB

1 1/2 teaspoons ground cumin

2 teaspoons chili powder

2 teaspoons grated orange zest

1 1/2 teaspoons dried sage

3/4 teaspoon kosher salt

3/4 teaspoon freshly ground pepper

STUFFING

6 ounces fresh white goat cheese at room temperature

3 tablespoons finely chopped Anaheim chili

1 1/2 teaspoons white wine Worcestershire sauce or regular Worcestershire sauce

1 green onion, including light green parts, finely chopped

Light a fire in a charcoal grill or preheat a gas grill to medium. (You can also use an oiled grill pan over medium heat.)

With a small, sharp knife, cut a pocket horizontally into the middle of each chop, pushing the knife all the way through to the bone.

TO MAKE THE SPICE RUB: In a small bowl, combine the ingredients and stir to blend. Divide the rub evenly on both sides of the chops and rub in.

TO MAKE THE STUFFING: In a small bowl, combine all the ingredients. Stuff the chops evenly with this mixture. Insert a toothpick into each chop to close the opening.

TO MAKE THE SAUCE: In a large sauté pan or skillet, heat the oil over medium heat. Add the leeks, garlic, chipotle, sage, and cumin, and sauté for 5 to 6 minutes. Add the red wine and cook to reduce by half. Add the stock, bring to a boil over high heat, then reduce heat to medium and simmer until reduced by half. Stir in the cornstarch mixture to thicken slightly. Remove from heat and swirl in the butter. Season with salt. Set aside and keep warm.

LEEK-CHIPOTLE SAUCE

1 1/2 tablespoons olive oil

2 leeks, including light green parts, rinsed and chopped

4 cloves garlic, minced

1 chipotle chili en adobo, drained and chopped

3/4 teaspoon dried sage

3/4 teaspoon ground cumin

1 1/2 cups dry red wine

2 1/2 cups low-salt chicken stock

1/2 teaspoon cornstarch mixed with 1/2 teaspoon cold water

2 tablespoons unsalted butter

Kosher salt

Flat-leaf parsley sprigs for garnish

Place the chops on the grill rack or in a grill pan and cook for 10 to 12 minutes. Very carefully turn chops so that the melted cheese does not run out. Cook 5 or 6 minutes longer on the second side.

To serve, spoon the sauce onto each warmed plate. Place a chop on top of the sauce. Remove the toothpicks. Garnish with parsley.

~Serves 6 as an entrée~

Pork Chops Stuffed with Stilton, Currants, and Pistachios, with Port Sauce

Recommended wine:
Cabernet

Alternative wine:
Merlot

The classic combination of Stilton and port was the inspiration for this flavorful dish. A ripe, fairly intense California Cabernet Sauvignon or a full-flavored Merlot will match well with the port sauce and the stuffing. Serve with a purée of sweet potatoes and carrots.

MARINADE

3 tablespoons olive oil or roasted garlic olive oil

1 1/2 teaspoons cumin seeds, toasted and crushed (see note, page 41)

1/2 teaspoon mustard seeds, toasted and crushed (see note, page 41)

2 1/2 teaspoons herbes de Provence or dried thyme

1/2 teaspoon kosher salt

1/4 teaspoon freshly ground pepper

Pinch of red pepper flakes

6 boneless pork loin chops (about 2 3/4 pounds total)

STUFFING

3/4 cup (4 ounces) finely crumbled Stilton or other blue cheese

1 1/2 tablespoons chopped green onion

3 tablespoons dried currants

2 tablespoons olive oil or roasted-garlic olive oil

TO MAKE THE MARINADE: In a small bowl, combine all the ingredients and mix well. Rub the marinade all over the pork. Place the pork in a large baking dish. Cover and refrigerate at least 3 hours or up to 5 hours.

Remove the pork from the refrigerator 30 minutes before cooking. Preheat the oven to 375°F.

TO MAKE THE STUFFING: In a small bowl, combine all the ingredients. Mix thoroughly and set aside.

TO MAKE THE SAUCE: In a large sauté pan or skillet, heat the 1/4 cup oil over medium heat. Add the red onions, garlic, shallot, carrots, and celery, and sauté until the onions are soft, 7 to 8 minutes. Add the 2 cups port, the red wine, and stock. Reduce heat to medium-low and cook to reduce until thickened. Strain the sauce, pushing down hard on the vegetables with the back of a large spoon to extract their flavor. Return the sauce to the pan. Add the 1 tablespoon port and simmer briefly. Remove from heat and stir in the butter 1 tablespoon at a time. Season with salt and pepper. Set aside and keep warm.

In a large, ovenproof sauté pan or skillet, heat the 2 tablespoons oil over medium heat until the surface shimmers. Sauté the pork, in batches if necessary, until browned, 3 to 4 minutes on each side.

CONTINUED

CONTINUED

Pork Chops Stuffed with Stilton, Currants, and Pistachios, with Port Sauce
(CONTINUED)

STUFFING (CONTINUED)

1 1/4 teaspoons dry white wine or Worcestershire sauce

1/4 cup pistachios, coarsely chopped

PORT SAUCE

1/4 cup olive oil

2 red onions, finely chopped

3 cloves garlic, minced

1 large shallot, minced

2 carrots, peeled and chopped

2 celery stalks, diced

2 cups ruby port, plus 1 tablespoon

2 cups dry red wine

1 3/4 cups low-salt beef or chicken stock

3 tablespoons cold unsalted butter, cut into 3 pieces

Kosher salt and freshly ground pepper

2 tablespoons olive oil

Transfer to a cutting board and cut a horizontal pocket in the end of each chop. Divide the stuffing evenly among the pockets. Place 2 toothpicks vertically into each chop at the opening to hold it closed. Return chop to the same pan and bake in the oven until opaque throughout, 12 to 14 minutes. Remove from the oven and remove the toothpicks from the chops.

To serve, divide the warm sauce evenly among 6 warmed plates. Place 1 chop on the sauce on each plate.

~Serves 6 as an entrée~

Roasted Pork Tenderloin with Spicy Orange-Port Reduction

Port wine—a magical ingredient in its own right—is used in this recipe as the foundation for a spicy marinade. The marinade serves as a roasting liquid for the tenderloin, and the pan juices then become the foundation for a spicy orange reduction sauce. Serve this with a cinnamon-scented couscous. A juicy Zinfandel or a full-bodied Merlot are winning choices at the table.

Recommended wine:
Zinfandel

Alternative wine:
Merlot

Grated zest and juice of 5 small Valencia or blood oranges (about 1 cup juice)

1 shallot, minced

3/4 tablespoon minced fresh thyme, or 1/2 teaspoon dried thyme

1/3 cup tawny or ruby port, plus 3 tablespoons

1 tablespoon balsamic vinegar

1 chipotle chili en adobo, drained and chopped (adobo sauce reserved)

3 tablespoons olive oil

3/4 teaspoon kosher salt

2 pork tenderloins (about 2 1/2 pounds total)

1/3 cup low-salt chicken stock

1/4 teaspoon cornstarch mixed with 1/4 teaspoon cold water

Thyme sprigs and orange slices for garnish

In a large bowl, combine all but 1 tablespoon of the orange zest, 3/4 cup of the orange juice, the shallot, thyme, the 1/3 cup port, the vinegar, chipotle chili, 1 1/2 tablespoons of the oil, and the salt. Whisk thoroughly. Transfer to a large baking dish, add the tenderloins, and turn to coat on all sides. Cover and refrigerate for at least 1 or up to 2 hours, turning once halfway through.

Preheat the oven to 400°F. Remove the tenderloins from the marinade and pat dry. Reserve the marinade.

In a heavy skillet over medium-high heat, heat the remaining 1 1/2 tablespoons oil over medium-high heat until the surface shimmers. Add the tenderloins and brown on all sides, 2 to 3 minutes. Carefully add the marinade to the pan, transfer to the oven, and roast until faintly pink in the center, 10 to 12 minutes. Transfer to a plate and cover loosely with aluminum foil.

To the same pan, add the 3 tablespoons port, the chicken stock, the remaining 1/4 cup juice, and the cornstarch mixture. Return the pan to the stove and reduce the liquid to a sauce. Strain the sauce, pressing on the solids. Taste and adjust the seasoning.

To serve, cut the pork into thin slices. Divide the sauce evenly among warmed plates and top with the pork slices. Sprinkle with the reserved 1 tablespoon zest. Garnish with the thyme sprigs and orange slices.

~*Serves 6 as an entrée*~

Fennel and Jack–Stuffed Veal Chops with Mushroom Orzo and Curry Sauce

Recommended wine:
Riesling

Alternative wine:
Pinot Gris

Curry scents both the stuffing and the sauce for these chops. A wine with lower alcohol and less oak is advised for cooking and for serving with curry-spiced dishes, so that it enhances and doesn't detract from the curry flavors. For drinking, fruity Riesling—totally lacking oak and bright with acidity and fruit—will echo the sauce, while Pinot Gris will offer a bit more roundness. Serve this dish with baby carrots.

2 large veal loin chops

Kosher salt and freshly ground pepper

FENNEL AND JACK STUFFING

1 tablespoon olive oil

1 cup chopped fennel

3 green onions, including light green parts, finely chopped

1 teaspoon Madras curry powder

1/2 cup grated dry Monterey Jack cheese

Kosher salt and freshly ground pepper

4 ounces oyster mushrooms

1 tablespoon olive oil

1/4 teaspoon Madras curry powder

Kosher salt and freshly ground pepper

Cut a pocket horizontally to the bone in the end of each chop. Sprinkle the chops with salt and pepper.

TO MAKE THE STUFFING: In a medium sauté pan or skillet, heat the oil over medium heat. Add the fennel, onions, and curry powder and sauté until the onions are translucent, 6 or 7 minutes. Add the cheese and stir just until melted. Season with salt and pepper. Transfer to a bowl and let cool. Stuff the chops and hold them together with toothpicks.

Preheat the oven to 350°F. In a small bowl, combine the mushrooms, olive oil, curry powder, and salt and pepper to taste. Toss to coat. Spread on a baking sheet and roast for 18 to 20 minutes, or until lightly browned. Remove from the oven. Set aside and keep warm.

Increase the oven temperature to 450°F. Put the veal chops in a roasting pan and roast until medium-rare, 17 to 19 minutes. Remove from the oven.

MEANWHILE, MAKE THE SAUCE: In a medium sauté pan or skillet, heat the olive oil over medium heat. Add the ginger, garlic, onion, and curry powder and sauté for 5 minutes. Add the wine, bring to a boil, then reduce heat to medium-low and cook to reduce by half. Stir in the stock, coconut milk, and chili paste. Cook to reduce by half again. Set aside and keep warm.

CURRY SAUCE

1 tablespoon olive oil

2 tablespoons minced fresh ginger

2 cloves garlic, minced

1/4 cup chopped yellow onion

1 teaspoon Madras curry powder

1/4 cup Riesling or Pinot Gris wine

1/2 cup low-salt chicken or vegetable stock

1 cup light coconut milk

1/4 teaspoon Thai chili paste

1/2 cup orzo

Flat-leaf parsley sprigs for garnish

While the chops are roasting, cook the orzo in a large pot of salted boiling water until al dente, 8 to 10 minutes. Drain and return to the pot. Chop the mushrooms and add to the orzo.

To serve, divide the orzo between 2 warmed plates. Pool the sauce next to the orzo and place a veal chop on top of the sauce. Garnish with parsley.

~Serves 2 as an entrée~

Sautéed Veal Loin with Thyme-Scented Caramelized Leeks

Recommended wine:
Pinot Noir

Alternative wine:
Merlot

Caramelizing any member of the allium family—onions, leeks, shallots, or garlic—converts their sugar into an intense flavor. Deglazing the sauté pan adds even more flavor to a sauce. A young California Pinot Noir or Washington state Merlot is a pleasing accompaniment. Serve with wild rice and butter-glazed cherry tomatoes.

1 tablespoon olive oil

1/2 tablespoon Dijon mustard

2 teaspoons minced fresh thyme, or 1 teaspoon dried thyme

Kosher salt and freshly ground pepper

2 rib-eye veal chops (about 1 1/2 pounds total), trimmed and boned, or 2 veal loins

THYME-SCENTED CARAMELIZED LEEKS

2 tablespoons unsalted butter

2 leeks, including light green parts, cleaned and thinly sliced

2 teaspoons minced fresh thyme, or 1 teaspoon dried thyme

1/4 cup dry white wine

Kosher salt and freshly ground pepper

1/2 tablespoon olive oil

1/2 cup dry red wine

1 cup low-salt beef or chicken stock

In a small bowl, combine the oil, mustard, thyme, and salt and pepper to taste and whisk thoroughly. Rub the mixture evenly on both sides of the chops. Set aside.

TO MAKE THE LEEKS: In a medium sauté pan or skillet, melt the butter over medium heat. Add the leeks and thyme. Sauté until the leeks are tender and browned, 16 to 18 minutes. Add the white wine and cook to reduce by half. Season with salt and pepper. Set aside and keep warm.

Preheat the oven to 400°F. In a large, ovenproof sauté pan or skillet, heat the oil over medium-high heat. Add the veal and cook until browned on the bottom, 6 to 7 minutes. Turn and cook until browned on the second side, 4 to 5 minutes. Put the pan in the oven and roast until medium-rare, about 5 minutes. Do not overcook. Remove from the oven and transfer chops to a plate. Cover loosely with aluminum foil and set aside.

Set the same pan over medium heat, add the red wine, and stir to scrape up the browned bits from the bottom of the pan. Cook to reduce by half. Add the stock and cook to reduce until thickened. Taste and adjust the seasoning.

To serve, spoon the warm leeks onto warmed plates. Place the veal on top of the leeks and spoon the pan sauce over the top.

~Serves 2 as an entrée~

Grilled Venison Loin with Sun-Dried Cherry and Cabernet Reduction

I've always had a fondness for venison, which is low in fat and cholesterol and high in flavor. Cabernet Sauvignon, with its cherry and currant fruit flavors, makes a perfect marinade and reduction sauce for the juicy, rare meat. If venison is not available, pork tenderloin is a good alternative; grill it for about 2 to 3 minutes longer on each side. Serve this dish with a sweet potato–carrot purée or dilled carrots and green beans.

Recommended wine:
Cabernet Sauvignon

Alternative wine:
Zinfandel

MARINADE

3/4 cup Cabernet Sauvignon or Zinfandel wine

1 1/2 tablespoons minced shallots

1 clove garlic, thinly sliced

6 juniper berries, crushed

4 whole cloves

1 teaspoon Dijon mustard

1 tablespoon olive oil

1/8 teaspoon kosher salt

1/8 teaspoon freshly ground pepper

1 1/2 to 1 3/4 pounds loin of venison

1 2/3 cups low-salt beef, veal, or chicken stock

1/2 cup sun-dried cherries

1/4 cup Cabernet Sauvignon or Zinfandel wine

2 tablespoons cold unsalted butter

TO MAKE THE MARINADE: In a small bowl, combine all the ingredients and whisk thoroughly. Transfer to a sealable plastic bag and put the venison in the bag. Turn the bag to coat the meat evenly. Refrigerate for at least 3 hours or up to 4 hours.

Light a fire in a charcoal grill or preheat a gas grill to high. (You can also use an oiled grill pan heated over high heat.)

Remove the venison from the refrigerator 30 minutes before cooking. Remove from the marinade, reserving the marinade, and pat dry with paper towels. Transfer the marinade to a large saucepan and bring to a simmer. Skim the grayish solids from the liquid. Add the stock, cherries, and wine. Cook to reduce by more than half. Remove from heat and swirl in the butter 1 tablespoon at a time. Set aside and keep warm.

Place the venison on the grill rack or in the grill pan and cook on one side for 4 to 5 minutes. Turn and grill for 3 to 4 minutes for rare. (Venison should not be overcooked or it will become "livery" tasting.)

To serve, spoon the warm sauce and cherries onto 4 warmed plates. Slice the venison thinly and place on top of the sauce.

~Serves 4 as an entrée~

Loin of Lamb with Rosemary–Green Peppercorn Sauce

This is a delicious adaptation of a recipe from Caprial Pence, a well-known chef from the Pacific Northwest, who currently owns Caprial's Bistro in Portland. The sauce is sparked with fresh rosemary and the tart taste of green peppercorns. Pork tenderloins may be substituted for the lamb; grill them for 7 to 8 minutes on each side. The peppery flavor of a California Cabernet Sauvignon or Syrah will underscore the peppercorns in the sauce. Serve this dish with roasted sweet potatoes and green beans.

> *Recommended wine:*
> **Cabernet Sauvignon**
>
> *Alternative wine:*
> **Syrah/Shiraz**

2 pounds lamb tenderloins (or loins cut from chops) or pork tenderloin

4 teaspoons extra-virgin olive oil

1 tablespoon country-style or regular Dijon mustard

6 sprigs rosemary, plus rosemary sprigs for garnish

3 cloves garlic, thinly sliced

Kosher salt and freshly ground pepper

ROSEMARY–GREEN PEPPERCORN SAUCE

1 tablespoon olive oil

3 large cloves garlic, minced

1 large shallot, minced

1 tablespoon minced fresh rosemary

2 cups dry red wine

4 1/2 cups rich lamb, beef, or veal stock

2 teaspoons chopped green peppercorns

1/2 cup heavy cream (optional)

Kosher salt and freshly ground pepper

Put the lamb loins in a baking dish. Drizzle with the oil and spread mustard evenly over the loins. Place the 6 rosemary sprigs and sliced garlic on top and sprinkle with salt and pepper. Let sit at room temperature for up to 2 hours.

Light a fire in a charcoal grill, or preheat a gas grill to medium-high. (You can also use an oiled grill pan over high heat.)

TO MAKE THE SAUCE: In a large sauté pan or skillet, heat the oil over medium heat. Add the garlic, shallot, and 1/2 tablespoon of the minced rosemary. Sauté until lightly browned, 2 to 3 minutes. Add the wine and bring to a simmer. Cook to reduce the wine by half. Add the stock, peppercorns, and cream (if using) and simmer until reduced by half. Strain the sauce and return to the pan. Add the remaining minced rosemary and simmer for 1 to 2 minutes. Season with salt and pepper. Set aside and keep warm.

Remove the rosemary and garlic from the lamb. Place the lamb on the grill rack or in the grill pan and cook for 2 to 3 minutes on one side. Turn and cook for 1 to 2 minutes on the second side for medium-rare. Cover loosely with aluminum foil and let rest for about 5 minutes.

To serve, spoon the sauce onto warmed plates. Slice the lamb and place on top. Garnish with rosemary sprigs.

~*Serves 6 as an entrée*~

Adobo-Grilled Filet Mignon with Red Bean Ragout

Recommended wine:
Syrah/Shiraz

Alternative wine:
Cabernet Sauvignon

Adapted from a recipe by Florida chef Allen Susser of Chef Allen's, this Latin American–influenced beef dish incorporates red wine in a sofrito, a flavor base for the ragout. The complexity of the ragout balances the robust flavors of the filet mignon. A hearty Syrah/Shiraz echoes the intensity of the dish. Serve this with corn on the cob.

SPICE PASTE

4 cloves garlic

1 teaspoon sea salt

1 teaspoon peppercorns

2 teaspoons minced fresh ginger

2 teaspoons minced fresh oregano

2 teaspoons chopped fresh cilantro

1 1/2 teaspoons ground cumin

2 tablespoons olive oil

Four 6-ounce filet mignon steaks

1 cup dried red beans, rinsed, picked over, and soaked overnight

TO MAKE THE SPICE PASTE: Using a large mortar and pestle, pound the garlic, salt, peppercorns, ginger, oregano, cilantro, and cumin into a paste. Add the olive oil and stir until incorporated. Rub the mixture into the filets. Cover and refrigerate for at least 2 hours or up to 4 hours.

Drain the beans and put them in a medium saucepan. Add water to cover by 2 inches. Bring to a boil, reduce heat, cover, and cook until tender, about 1 1/2 hours. Drain and set aside.

TO MAKE THE SOFRITO: In a large sauté pan or skillet, sauté the pancetta over medium heat for 3 to 4 minutes. Add the Anaheim chili, tomato, onion, oregano, cilantro, and cumin, and sauté for 5 minutes. Add the red wine and simmer until most of the liquid is evaporated, 6 to 8 minutes.

Add the beans and squash to the sofrito, cover, and cook until the squash is tender, about 25 minutes. Add the lime juice and simmer for several minutes. Season with salt and pepper.

SOFRITO

4 ounces pancetta, chopped

1 Anaheim chili, seeded and diced

1 tomato, seeded and diced
(see note, page 68)

1 onion, diced

1 teaspoon chopped fresh oregano

1 teaspoon chopped fresh cilantro

1 teaspoon ground cumin

1/2 cup dry red wine

1 cup 1-inch cubed winter squash
or calabaza

3 tablespoons fresh lime juice

Kosher salt and freshly ground
pepper

Cilantro sprigs for garnish

Meanwhile, light a fire in a charcoal grill, or preheat a gas grill to high. (You may also use an oiled grill pan heated over high heat.) Place the filets on the grill rack or in the grill pan and cook until well crusted on the bottom, 5 to 6 minutes. Turn and grill on the second side for 4 to 5 minutes for medium-rare.

To serve, spoon the warm beans onto warmed plates. Top with the filets and garnish with cilantro sprigs.

~Serves 4 as an entrée~

Seared Peppercorn and Spice–Crusted Rib-Eye
with Roquefort and Walnuts

Recommended wine:
Syrah or Australian Shiraz

Alternative wine:
Zinfandel

I love a good pepper steak. This version features a spicy crust and red-wine pan sauce. The peppery fruit and roundness of Syrah/Shiraz are ideal for this full-flavored dish. Serve with potato gratin and stuffed zucchini.

1 tablespoon mixed peppercorns

1 tablespoon cumin seed

1 tablespoon mustard seed

1 teaspoon kosher salt

4 boneless rib-eye steaks (about 2 1/2 pounds total) at room temperature

1 teaspoon olive oil or roasted-garlic olive oil

SAUCE

1 shallot, minced

1 tablespoon tomato paste

3/4 cup dry red wine

3/4 cup low-salt beef or chicken stock

1 tablespoon balsamic vinegar

3 tablespoons cold unsalted butter, cut into small pieces

Kosher salt

GARNISH

3 tablespoons crumbled Roquefort cheese

3 tablespoons coarsely chopped walnuts, toasted (see note, page 35)

1 tablespoon minced fresh chives

In a mortar or a spice grinder, combine the peppercorns, cumin seed, mustard seed, and salt, and grind thoroughly. Coat the steaks thoroughly with oil, then rub with the spice mixture.

Heat a heavy sauté pan or skillet over high heat for 2 to 3 minutes. Add the steaks to the dry pan, leaving some space between them. Reduce heat to medium-high and sear the steaks on one side for 4 minutes. Flip the steaks and cook for 3 minutes on the second side for medium-rare. Transfer the steaks to a plate and cover loosely with aluminum foil.

TO MAKE THE SAUCE: In the same pan over medium heat, sauté the shallot and tomato paste for about 2 minutes. Increase heat to medium-high and gradually stir in the wine, stock, and balsamic vinegar. Cook to reduce the liquid by about a third. Strain the sauce and whisk in the butter and salt.

To serve, divide the sauce evenly among 4 warmed plates and place the steaks on top. Sprinkle the Roquefort over the steaks and top with walnuts and chives.

~Serves 4 as an entrée~

Steaming

Wine is incredibly versatile in cooking. Although its most obvious uses are in marinades and reduction sauces, it can also be an important element in steaming.

Steamed dishes rely on moist heat to cook food that is placed above it in a steamer basket, or when the food rests just above the liquid (see Pan Stew of Shellfish and Tomatoes, page 68). Wine is employed to make a simple court-bouillon with aromatic vegetables, or it may be part of a more highly seasoned steaming liquid. Steaming is one of the most healthful ways to cook, since no fat is required for the process.

The cooking liquid is first brought to the boiling point and the pot is covered to trap the moist heat and the flavors of the food. A tight lid is required in order to retain the moist heat and flavors of the food.

Steaming is a particularly effective way to cook bivalves such as mussels and clams, as the heat causes the shells to open, allowing the aroma of the steaming liquid to infuse the meat while juices are released into the cooking liquid. The liquid can then be reduced to provide a wondrously tasty broth in which to serve the shellfish. Steaming other shellfish, including crab and lobster, is an excellent way to keep it extremely moist.

Another excellent way to steam fish is *en papillote:* enclosing it in a packet of parchment paper or aluminum foil and baking it in the oven. The flavors that result from this process are very intense and the fish emerges moist and tender. Greek-Style Shrimp with Retsina and Feta (page 121) is a good example: The shrimp are infused with the slightly bitter, resinlike flavor of retsina, while the salty feta melts magnificently.

Skinless chicken breasts can be steamed as well, though this takes a good deal more cooking liquid.

STEAMING

RECOMMENDED WINES FOR STEAMING

WINE	FOOD
Sauvignon/Fumé Blanc	Mussels, clams, crab, shrimp
Pinot Gris/Pinot Grigio	Mussels, clams, crab, shrimp
Vermouth	Crab
Sake	Mussels, clams
Mirin	Mussels, clams
Marsala	Chicken
Retsina	Shrimp

TIPS ON STEAMING WITH WINE

- Make sure that the pot is tightly fitted with a lid so that no heat or aromatics escape.

- The preferred wines for steaming are Sauvignon/Fumé Blanc, Pinot Gris/Pinot Grigio, or in the case of Asian-style dishes, Riesling or Gewürztraminer.

- Add wine to a court-bouillon or with sautéed aromatic vegetables.

- Select a pot that is large enough to allow good circulation of steam around the food in order to cook it evenly.

- Use enough liquid to keep it from boiling away and scorching the bottom of the pot.

Steamed Mussels with Thai Curry Sauce

Aficionados of these glorious mollusks have been steaming them for years in white wine and fish stock to create simple but tasty preparations. In this version, that mixture is embellished with a Thai-style sauce that makes a wonderful "soup" for the mussels. A fruity Gewürztraminer or Riesling is recommended for both cooking and drinking to enhance the spicy Thai flavors.

Recommended wine:
Gewürztraminer

Alternative wine:
Riesling

1 tablespoon olive oil or unsalted butter

1 cup chopped yellow onions

1/4 cup minced peeled fresh ginger

2 cloves garlic, minced

1 tablespoon minced lemongrass

1 teaspoon minced lemon zest

2/3 cup Gewürztraminer or Riesling wine

2 cups low-salt fish stock or vegetable stock

2/3 cup light coconut milk

1 tablespoon Madras curry powder

2 1/2 teaspoons Thai chili paste

2 teaspoons Thai fish sauce

1 1/2 teaspoons fresh lemon juice

2 1/2 pounds mussels, scrubbed and debearded

3/4 cup chopped fresh cilantro

3 tablespoons finely chopped green onion, including light green parts

In a large soup pot, heat the oil or butter over medium heat. Add the chopped onions, ginger, garlic, lemongrass, and zest and sauté for 2 to 3 minutes. Add the wine, increase heat to high, and bring to a boil. Reduce heat to a simmer and cook until the liquid is nearly evaporated. Add the stock, coconut milk, curry powder, chili paste, fish sauce, and lemon juice, and simmer for 5 to 6 minutes.

Put the mussels in a steamer basket and set the basket in the soup pot. Cover and steam until the mussels open, 5 to 7 minutes. Discard any mussels that do not open. Using a slotted spoon, transfer the mussels to a bowl. Cook the liquid for 3 to 4 minutes to reduce it.

To serve, divide mussels and broth among warmed soup bowls. Garnish with the cilantro and green onion.

~Serves 4 to 6 as an appetizer, 2 to 3 as an entrée~

Pan Stew of Shellfish and Tomatoes

Recommended wine:
Pinot Gris/Pinot Grigio

Alternative wine:
Sauvignon/Fumé Blanc

This extraordinarily simple and tasty dish, adapted slightly from a recipe by Michael Chiarello, formerly of Tra Vigne restaurant in St. Helena, California, is a quick pan stew made with a dry white wine. A crisp Pinot Gris or Pinot Grigio is a complementary tablemate.

2 tablespoons extra-virgin olive oil

1 1/2 tablespoons sliced garlic

1 1/2 pounds mussels, scrubbed and debearded

1 cup dry white wine

Kosher salt and freshly ground pepper

3 large yellow tomatoes, peeled (see note) and cut into chunks the size of the mussels, or two 14 1/2-ounce cans of tomatoes, drained

1 tablespoon minced fresh purple or green basil

1 1/2 teaspoons minced fresh tarragon

1 1/2 teaspoons minced fresh flat-leaf parsley

1 tablespoon capers

2 tablespoons unsalted butter (optional)

In a large sauté pan or skillet, heat the olive oil over medium-high heat. Add the garlic and sauté just until light brown. Add the mussels, wine, and salt and pepper to taste. Bring to a simmer, stir, then cover and cook until the mussels open, about 3 minutes. Using a slotted spoon, transfer the mussels to a plate. Discard any mussels that do not open.

Cook the pan juices over medium-high heat to reduce by half. Add the tomatoes and cook until they begin to color the juice, about 30 seconds. Don't overcook, or they will break apart in the sauce. Add the herbs, capers, and butter, if using. Return the mussels to the pan. Stir and toss to reheat. Taste and adjust the seasoning. Serve immediately in soup bowls.

❖ NOTE: **To peel tomatoes,** cut a shallow X in the bottom end of the fruit. Blanch in boiling water for about 1 minute. Transfer to a bowl of cold water, then peel, using a paring knife. To seed tomatoes, cut out the stem, then halve the tomatoes crosswise. Hold each half over the sink and squeeze gently, shaking the tomato to release the seeds.

~Serves 4 as a first course, 2 as an entrée~

Spicy Dilled Prawns with Pepper Jack and Couscous

The prawns and couscous for this flavorful dish are steamed in foil bags. A bit of the same wine you're serving at the table is a logical choice to be used in the steaming liquid.

Recommended wine:
Sauvignon/Fumé Blanc

Alternative wine:
Pinot Gris/Pinot Grigio

1 tablespoon roasted garlic
(see note, page 33)

1 red bell pepper, roasted, peeled, and finely chopped (see note, page 33)

1/4 cup kalamata olives, pitted and chopped

1 cup diced tomatoes

1/4 cup finely chopped green onion, including light green parts

1/2 tablespoon grated lemon zest

2 tablespoons Sauvignon or Fumé Blanc wine

2 serrano chilies, seeded and minced

1/4 cup minced fresh dill, plus
1 tablespoon for garnish

1/3 cup crumbled pepper Jack cheese

1 tablespoon olive oil

1/4 teaspoon kosher salt

1/8 teaspoon cayenne pepper, or
1/4 teaspoon sauce from canned chipotles en adobo

12 ounces jumbo prawns, shelled and deveined

1 cup cooked couscous

Preheat the oven to 450°F. In a large bowl, combine the roasted garlic, roasted bell pepper, olives, tomatoes, green onion, zest, wine, chilies, the 1/4 cup dill, the cheese, olive oil, salt, and cayenne or adobo sauce. Whisk thoroughly. Add the prawns and toss to coat.

Spray the inside of 2 small aluminum foil bags with cooking spray. Divide the couscous between them. Divide the prawn mixture evenly on top of the couscous. Close the bags and place in a baking pan. Bake for 24 minutes, or until just heated through.

Cut the bags open with scissors and pull back the foil. Serve 1 on each plate. Sprinkle with the remaining dill.

~Serves 2 as an entrée~

Portuguese Steamed Clams with Sausage

Recommended wine:
Albariño

Alternative wine:
Viognier

Joyce Goldstein, my "kissin' cousin" and a truly great chef, has lent me this recipe, which I adapted from her landmark cookbook, *Mediterranean Kitchen.* The dish works equally well with mussels (you'll need about 2¼ pounds). Albariño is a white grape variety grown extensively in Spain; its aromatic character and intense fruitiness work well here. Serve this on a wintry Sunday night to warm the heart and soothe the soul.

12 ounces chorizo or linguiça sausage

¼ cup olive oil

2 red onions, thinly sliced

2 tablespoons minced garlic

1 tablespoon sweet Hungarian paprika

½ teaspoon red pepper flakes, or to taste

1 cup dry white wine

1 cup dry sherry

¾ cup fish or chicken stock

3 ½ cups diced peeled fresh tomatoes, or 3 cups canned tomatoes with their juices

3 ounces prosciutto, julienned

½ cup minced fresh flat-leaf parsley, plus more for garnish

2 bay leaves, crumbled

Kosher salt and freshly ground pepper

60 tiny Manila clams or 36 larger clams, scrubbed

Preheat the oven to 400°F. Prick the sausages with a fork, place in a roasting pan, and bake about 20 minutes, or until lightly browned. Remove from the pan and reserve the fat. Cut the sausage into 1-inch chunks.

In a large stockpot, heat the oil and the reserved sausage fat over medium heat. Add the onions and sauté for 10 minutes, or until very soft. Add the garlic, paprika, and red pepper flakes and cook for several more minutes. Stir in the wine, sherry, stock, tomatoes, prosciutto, the ½ cup minced parsley, the bay leaves, and sausage and simmer until thickened. Season with salt and pepper.

Bring the mixture to a boil. Add the clams, cover the pan, and steam until they open, 5 to 7 minutes. Discard any clams that do not open. Divide the clams and sauce evenly among large bowls and sprinkle with a little parsley.

~Serves 4 to 6 as an entrée~

Clams Steamed in Lemongrass and Ginger–Infused Sake

This simple, tasty Asian-influenced dish uses an exotic infusion of Japanese rice wine to steam the clams. Serve it with a crusty baguette for dipping into the sauce. Accompany with warm sake to mirror the flavors, or a lively Pinot Gris or Pinot Grigio to brighten the flavors with its crisp acidity.

> Recommended wine:
> **Sake**
>
> Alternative wine:
> **Pinot Gris/Pinot Grigio**

1/3 cup sake

1 cup fish stock or clam juice

2 tablespoons minced fresh ginger

1 tablespoon minced lemongrass

2 cloves garlic, minced

4 tablespoons minced fresh basil

1/8 teaspoon red pepper flakes

Kosher salt

1 1/2 pounds clams, scrubbed

1 1/2 tablespoons cold unsalted butter

In a large steamer, combine the sake, stock or clam juice, ginger, lemongrass, garlic, 2 1/2 tablespoons of the basil, red pepper flakes, and salt to taste. Bring to a boil. Put the clams in a steamer basket, put it in the pot, and cover. Steam until the clams open, 5 to 7 minutes. Remove the pot from heat and discard any clams that do not open. Stir in the butter.

Using a slotted spoon, transfer the clams to bowls and pour the hot liquid over. Garnish with the remaining basil.

~Serves 4 as a first course, 2 as an entrée~

Steamed Shiitake and Spinach Wontons in Mirin Broth

Recommended wine:
Riesling

Alternative wine:
Gewürztraminer

Steaming wontons with a mirin-infused broth that becomes part of the finished dish is a sure-fire method to success. Mirin, a sweet rice wine, has a distinctive aroma and flavor that melds nicely with the spicy wontons. An off-dry Riesling from the Moselle, California, or Washington state would be an appropriate companion, as would a Gewürztraminer.

WONTONS

6 ounces fresh spinach leaves
(about 6 packed cups)

1 1/2 tablespoons olive oil

1 large clove garlic, minced

2 tablespoons minced fresh ginger

2 serrano chilies, minced

2 tablespoons minced fresh cilantro

6 ounces shiitake mushrooms,
stemmed and coarsely chopped

1 1/2 tablespoons mirin (see note,
page 74)

Kosher salt and freshly ground
pepper

14 round wonton skins

TO MAKE THE WONTONS: Cook the spinach in a pot of salted boiling water for 2 minutes. Empty into a colander and run cold water over the spinach, pressing on it with the back of a large spoon to remove all the moisture. Spread on paper towels and pat dry. Chop finely and set aside.

In a large sauté pan or skillet, heat the oil over medium-high heat. Add the garlic, ginger, chilies, and cilantro and sauté for 4 to 5 minutes. Add the mushrooms and mirin and sauté until the liquid has evaporated. Stir in the chopped spinach. Season with salt and pepper. Remove from heat and let cool.

Place the wonton skins on a well-oiled baking sheet. Spoon 2 teaspoons spinach mixture in a mound in the center of each wonton. Wet the outer rim of the wonton with your fingers. Pull the top side down over the mixture and seal onto the bottom part. Lightly spray the wontons with vegetable-oil cooking spray.

CONTINUED

CONTINUED

Steamed Shiitake and Spinach Wontons in Mirin Broth (CONTINUED)

BROTH

1/4 cup mirin

3/4 cup dry white wine

1 large shallot, minced

1 1/2 tablespoons rice vinegar

1 teaspoon plum sauce (see note)

3 teaspoons low-salt soy sauce

2 tablespoons cold unsalted butter

GARNISH

Cilantro sprigs

1 *each* yellow and red bell pepper, roasted, peeled, and chopped (see note, page 33)

TO MAKE THE BROTH: In a large steamer, combine all the ingredients and bring to a gentle simmer. Put the wontons in a steamer basket, add to the steamer, cover, and cook until heated through, 3 to 4 minutes.

Divide the wontons evenly among 4 soup bowls. Pour the liquid over. Garnish with the cilantro sprigs and bell peppers.

❈ NOTE: **Mirin and plum sauce** can be found in Asian markets or the Asian sections of better grocery stores.

~Serves 4 as an appetizer~

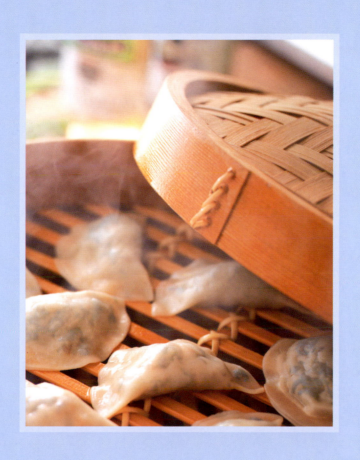

Simmering and Poaching

Simmering, more than its more aggressive big brother boiling, is an effective and versatile way to use wine in cooking. This chapter focuses on dishes using wine that has been reduced by simmering, as well as those in which wine is a key ingredient in a poaching liquid.

Simmering wine reduces it to more syrupy consistency and concentrates its flavors while evaporating the alcohol. *Simmering* means to bring a liquid to a temperature that is below a rolling boil; a simmer can be brisk, or low, i.e. barely moving. *Poaching* means to cook food in liquid brought to a low simmer.

When wine is simmered, it's important to moderate the heat so that the wine doesn't splatter on the sides of the pot and burn. First, bring the wine to a gentle boil, which will burn off the alcohol, then immediately reduce the heat to a simmer. Depending on the recipe, some cooks add a bit of sugar or honey to the wine in order to balance its acidity and mollify its astringency (see Prosciutto with Peaches, Zinfandel, and Sweet Onion Salad, page 88).

One of the favorite uses of the simmering process is in the preparation of risotto, for which there are several recipes in this chapter. An initial addition of wine provides an acidity that balances the creamy richness of Arborio or Carnaroli rice.

Poaching is a delicate technique most commonly used with fish, poultry, and tender meats to keep the meat moist and cook it evenly. Most poaching liquids are made up of some combination of water, fish fumet, wine, lemon juice, vinegar, and court-bouillon (an aromatic mixture of wine, water, and vegetables). The key to poaching is the full immersion of the food in the cooking liquid, with enough room in the pot for the liquid to circulate easily.

Many poaching recipes call for starting fish or chicken in a cold poaching liquid, which cooks the exterior and interior evenly and helps to prevent fish, in particular, from falling apart. Leftover poaching liquid can be cooled and refrigerated or frozen to use as a base for soups or sauces. Because of the relatively diluted form of most poaching liquids, it's often necessary to reduce them or add demi-glace for flavor.

SIMMERING AND POACHING

TIPS ON SIMMERING AND POACHING WITH WINE

Make sure to simmer, not boil, wine slowly, to keep it from splattering on the sides of the pot and burning.

Freeze reduced wine in ice cube trays for easy access and addition to sauces.

If reduced wine is too tart, balance it with sugar or honey.

Dry red wines such as Merlot, Zinfandel, Pinot Noir, Syrah/Shiraz, and Cabernet Sauvignon add tartness and structure to foods, while fruity whites such as Sauvignon/Fumé Blanc add delicate flavor. Slightly sweet wines will add a hint of sweetness to the finished dish.

When poaching, make sure not to boil the liquid; it should be kept at a very low simmer.

When making soups, reduce the wine first to burn off the alcohol, then add it to the stock.

When making risotto, wine is first simmered and thoroughly reduced with the rice until it's completely absorbed and the alcohol burns off. After this takes place, a series of reductions with hot stock will swell the rice to its perfect al dente state.

A splash of wine added to the pan at the end of cooking a risotto can help unite its flavors.

Caramelized Onion and Jalapeño Waffles with Smoked Salmon, Radish Salad, and Lemon Cream

Recommended wine:
Champagne/Sparking Wine

Alternative wine:
Riesling

This elegant first course or brunch dish was created by San Francisco caterer Richard Crocker. Here, it has been adapted by adding Champagne or sparkling wine to the caramelized onions. Serve this with Champagne mimosas for brunch—or with Champagne as a first course. A slightly sweet Riesling is also complementary.

CARAMELIZED ONIONS

3 tablespoons unsalted butter

2 yellow onions, finely diced

1 jalapeño chili, seeded and minced

3 tablespoons Champagne or sparkling wine

LEMON CREAM

1 cup sour cream

1/4 cup milk

Grated zest of 1 lemon

5 tablespoons fresh lemon juice

1/2 teaspoon kosher salt

1 teaspoon sugar

RADISH SALAD

8 ounces mixed salad greens

2 bunches radishes, trimmed and thinly sliced

3 green onions, including light green parts, finely chopped

5 tablespoons fresh lemon juice

2 tablespoons extra-virgin olive oil

1 1/2 teaspoons Dijon mustard

Kosher salt and freshly ground pepper

TO MAKE THE ONIONS: In a large sauté pan or skillet, melt the butter over medium heat. Add the onions and jalapeño and sauté until the onions are caramelized, 8 to 10 minutes. Add the wine and simmer until thoroughly reduced. Set aside.

TO MAKE THE CREAM: In a medium bowl, combine all the ingredients and whisk to blend. Cover and refrigerate.

TO MAKE THE SALAD: In a medium salad bowl, combine the salad greens, radishes, and green onions. In a small nonmetal mixing bowl, combine the lemon juice, olive oil, mustard, and salt and pepper to taste. Whisk to blend. Cover and refrigerate.

TO MAKE THE WAFFLES: In a large bowl, combine the flour, herbs, baking powder, pepper, and salt. Stir to blend. In a separate bowl, combine the milk, eggs, and clarified butter and whisk thoroughly. Fold the wet ingredients into the dry ingredients just until moistened. The batter should be slightly lumpy. Fold in the caramelized onion mixture.

Heat a waffle iron according to the manufacturer's instructions. Spray with vegetable-oil cooking spray. Cook the waffle batter, being careful not to overfill the iron, until golden brown, 6 to 7 minutes. Transfer to a plate and keep warm in a low oven while cooking the remaining batter. Stir the batter and oil the iron before cooking each batch to prevent sticking.

WAFFLES

2 cups all-purpose flour

1/2 cup mixed minced fresh herbs, such as parsley, thyme, chives

1 1/2 tablespoons baking powder

1/2 teaspoon freshly ground pepper

1 teaspoon kosher salt

1 1/2 cups milk

2 eggs at room temperature, beaten

1/3 cup clarified butter, melted

4 ounces thinly sliced gravlax or smoked salmon, or 4 ounces caviar for garnish (optional)

To serve, place 2 waffle squares slightly overlapping in the center of each plate. Roll the gravlax or smoked salmon (if using) into tubes and place them beside the waffles. Toss the salad with the dressing and top each waffle with a salad portion. Drizzle the entire plate with lemon cream. If using caviar, dollop a tiny amount into the lemon cream.

~Serves 6 to 8 as a first course or brunch entrée~

Grilled Asparagus with Ginger and Black Bean Vinaigrette

Recommended wine:
Gewürztraminer

Alternative wine:
Sauvignon/Fumé Blanc

Reduced mirin is a primary contributor to this full-flavored Asian vinaigrette, adding a sweet edge to its spicy, salty, and tart flavors. A slightly sweet Gewürztraminer or crisp, fruity, lightly oaked Sauvignon/Fumé Blanc will flatter the zippy vinaigrette.

24 asparagus stalks, trimmed

8 ounces shiitake mushrooms, stemmed

2 tablespoons olive oil

GINGER AND BLACK BEAN VINAIGRETTE

1/2 cup mirin (see note, page 74) or sweet white vermouth

2 1/2 tablespoons minced pickled ginger (see note)

2 teaspoons minced shallot

2 tablespoons low-salt soy sauce

5 tablespoons seasoned rice vinegar

1 1/2 teaspoons Chinese fermented black bean sauce (see note)

1/4 cup canola oil

1 tablespoon sesame chili oil

Splash of fresh lemon juice

Kosher salt and freshly ground pepper

4 ounces mixed baby greens

1 bunch red radishes, trimmed and sliced

1/2 tablespoon sesame seeds, toasted (see note, page 41), for garnish

In a large pot of salted boiling water, blanch the asparagus until crisp-tender, 5 to 6 minutes. Place in an ice bath to cool, then drain again and pat dry with paper towels. Lightly oil a grill pan and heat over medium-high heat. Cook the asparagus until lightly browned. Transfer to a plate. Put the mushrooms in a bowl and coat with the olive oil. Grill the mushrooms, turning frequently until browned, about 6 to 8 minutes.

TO MAKE THE VINAIGRETTE: In a small saucepan, simmer the mirin or vermouth to reduce it by half. In a small bowl, combine the ginger, shallot, soy sauce, vinegar, reduced mirin, and black bean sauce. Whisk thoroughly. Gradually whisk in both oils. Add the lemon juice and season with salt and pepper.

To serve, arrange the greens on salad plates. Place 6 asparagus spears on each plate. Vigorously whisk the vinaigrette and spoon it over the top. Garnish with radishes and sprinkle sesame seeds over the top of the asparagus. Place the mushrooms around the rims of the plates. Save any remaining vinaigrette for another use.

❖ NOTE: **Pickled ginger and Chinese black bean sauce** can be found in Asian markets and the Asian section of many supermarkets.

~Serves 4 as a first course~

Mediterranean-Style Eggplant "Tarts" with Black Olive Dressing

Recommended wine:
Sauvignon/Fumé Blanc

Alternative wine:
Zinfandel

Infusing sautéed leeks and garlic with white wine in these layered tarts (really "Napoleons" without the fanfare) adds a hint of sweet complexity to the mixture. Pesto, goat cheese, tomatoes, and olives add a Mediterranean flavor to this dish, perfect for alfresco dining. A slightly herbal California or New Zealand Sauvignon/Fumé Blanc will complement the goat cheese and tomatoes while contrasting with the salty olives. Zinfandel will robustly echo all the flavors.

1 large globe eggplant (about 1 1/4 pounds)

Kosher salt

Olive oil for brushing, plus 1 1/2 tablespoons

3 leeks, including light green parts

3 cloves garlic, minced

1/4 cup dry white wine

5 small vine-ripened tomatoes (about 1 pound), seeded and chopped (see note, page 68), plus diced fresh tomatoes for garnish

2 tablespoons chopped fresh basil, plus basil sprigs for garnish

3 tablespoons basil pesto (recipe follows)

1/3 cup crumbled fresh white goat cheese

1/4 cup oil-cured black olives, pitted and chopped

Freshly ground pepper

Reduced balsamic vinegar for garnish

Cut the eggplant into 8 fairly thin slices. Place on paper towels and sprinkle with salt on both sides. Let sweat for 30 minutes. Rinse and pat dry. Brush with olive oil on both sides. Cut the leeks into thin crosswise slices, rinse well, and drain.

Preheat the oven to 350°F. Put the eggplant slices on a baking sheet and bake until lightly browned, about 15 minutes. Set aside.

In a large sauté pan or skillet, heat the 1 1/2 tablespoons oil over medium heat. Add the leeks and garlic and sauté until the leeks begin to caramelize, 8 to 10 minutes. Add the wine, bring to a boil, then reduce heat and simmer until caramelized, about 4 minutes. Transfer to a large bowl and set aside.

Add the tomatoes and chopped basil to the same pan and sauté over medium heat for 3 to 4 minutes. Drain and reserve.

Preheat the oven to 400°F. Spread half of the pesto evenly over 4 of the largest eggplant slices. Divide the leek mixture evenly on top of the pesto, spreading it out to cover the eggplant evenly. Repeat with the tomato mixture, then sprinkle evenly with the goat cheese and olives. Season with salt and pepper to taste. Spread the remaining pesto on the 4 smaller pieces of eggplant and place these pieces, pesto-side down, on top of the other 4 stacks.

Place on a baking sheet and bake for 16 to 18 minutes, until just done. Let cool and serve at room temperature. Garnish with basil sprigs and sprinkle chopped tomatoes around the tarts. Drizzle the plates with the reduced balsamic vinegar.

~Serves 4 as an appetizer or lunch entrée~

PESTO

1 cup packed fresh basil leaves

3/4 tablespoon roasted or minced garlic or shallots

3 tablespoons pine nuts

1 tablespoon grated Parmesan cheese

1/2 cup extra-virgin olive oil

Kosher salt and freshly ground pepper

PESTO

In a blender or food processor, combine the basil leaves, garlic or shallots, pine nuts, Parmesan cheese, and olive oil. Process until smooth. Season with salt and pepper. Store in an airtight glass jar in the refrigerator for up to 2 weeks.   *~Makes 3/4 pint~*

Prosciutto with Peaches, Zinfandel, and Sweet Onion Salad

Recommended wine:
Riesling

Alternative wine:
Gewürztraminer

Jimmy Schmidt of Detroit's Rattlesnake Club is a master at cooking with wine. In this appealing appetizer, which has been adapted slightly from his recipe, Zinfandel, honey, and sweet onions are reduced to a syrup that becomes the basis for a dressing, while the remaining reduction garnishes the plate with a radiant dark red glow. Although Zinfandel would seem to be the obvious choice for pairing, an off-dry Riesling or Gewürztraminer is a better match with the dressing.

2 cups Zinfandel wine

2 tablespoons honey

1 cup thinly sliced sweet white onion (Vidalia, Walla Walla, or Maui)

2 to 3 tablespoons extra-virgin olive oil

Kosher salt and freshly ground pepper

1 fresh peach or nectarine, halved, pitted, cut into 1/8-inch-thick slices

1 bunch arugula, stemmed and cut into fine crosswise shreds

12 paper-thin slices Italian prosciutto (about 8 ounces)

4 large, paper-thin shavings Parmigiano-Reggiano cheese

In a small saucepan, combine the wine, honey, and onion slices. Bring to a boil over high heat, reduce heat to a simmer, and cook the mixture to reduce to a syrup, 10 to 12 minutes. Remove from heat and strain, pressing down on the onions with the back of a large spoon. Reserve the onions. Pour half of the liquid into a small bowl and reserve the remaining liquid, which can be used as a dressing for a salad at another meal. Whisk the olive oil into the liquid in the bowl. Season with salt and pepper. Set aside at room temperature.

In a medium bowl, combine the peach or nectarine and arugula. Add the dressing and toss to combine.

To serve, divide the prosciutto among 4 salad plates, overlapping them on one-half of each plate. Divide and mound the salad alongside the prosciutto. Divide the onions over the salad and prosciutto. Top with a cheese shaving. Sprinkle with a little freshly ground pepper.

~Serves 4 as a first course~

Caramelized Onion Soup with Gruyère Cheese Croutons

Ever since I was a kid and my mother started experimenting with French cooking, I've loved the sumptuous goodness of classic French onion soup. This recipe, adapted from one by Curtis de Carion of Café Esin in San Ramon, California, makes use of both red and white wine, along with brandy. The spirits give the sweet caramelized onions a ground of acidity and fruit, which are key to the success of the dish. Serve with a fruity Beaujolais—as would no doubt be done in a Parisian bistro—or an off-dry California or Washington state Riesling.

> **Recommended wine:**
> **Gamay (Beaujolais)**
>
> *Alternative wine:*
> **Riesling**

GRUYÈRE CHEESE CROUTONS

1 wide loaf sourdough bread

About 1/3 cup olive oil

2 cups (8 ounces) shredded Gruyère cheese

2 tablespoons unsalted butter

1 red onion, julienned

1 yellow onion, julienned

1 sweet white onion (Vidalia, Walla Walla, or Maui), julienned

1 teaspoon dried fines herbes

1 cup dry white wine

1 cup dry red wine

1/2 cup brandy

1 bay leaf

5 cups low-salt vegetable stock

Juice of 1/2 lemon

Kosher salt and freshly ground pepper

2 cups (8 ounces) shredded Gruyère cheese

Preheat the oven to 300°F.

TO MAKE CROUTONS: Cut the bread into six 3/4-inch-thick slices. Trim to fit inside the soup bowls, if necessary. Brush the bread on both sides with olive oil. Place on a baking sheet, top with the cheese, and bake in the oven until crisp all the way through, 50 to 60 minutes. Watch closely to prevent burning. Transfer to a wire rack and let cool.

In a large saucepan or skillet, melt the butter over medium heat until it foams. Add the onions and fines herbes. Reduce heat slightly and cook, stirring occasionally, until the onions are golden brown, 45 to 55 minutes. Increase heat and add the wines and brandy. Stir to scrape up the browned bits from the bottom of the pan. Cook to reduce until the liquid is almost completely evaporated. Add the bay leaf and stock and increase heat to medium-high. Cook until almost boiling. Reduce heat and simmer for 25 to 30 minutes. Add the lemon juice and season with salt and pepper. Remove the bay leaf. Keep warm or reheat before finishing in the oven.

To serve, preheat the broiler. Transfer the hot soup to ovenproof soup bowls, making sure that the onions and liquid are divided evenly. Top with the bread and evenly divide the cheese over the bread. Place under the broiler about 9 inches from the heat source until the cheese is bubbling and browned, 5 to 6 minutes. Serve immediately. Slurping is entirely permissible.

~Serves 6 as a hearty first course or a light entrée~

Goat Cheese Salad with Caramelized Red Onion–Merlot Dressing and Wine-Glazed Roasted Walnuts

The inspiration for this composed salad came from chef Daniel Bruce at Rowes Wharf at the Boston Harbor Hotel. The wine adds a pleasing tartness to the sweet onions, bitter walnuts, and creamy goat cheese. It's used in a dressing as well as in a glaze for the roasted walnuts. The hearty forward fruit of a good Merlot works well both in the recipe and as a table wine.

Recommended wine:
Merlot

Alternative wine:
Cabernet Sauvignon

CARAMELIZED RED ONION–MERLOT DRESSING

3 tablespoons olive oil, plus 1/4 cup

1 red onion, diced

3/4 teaspoon dried thyme

1 cup Merlot or other dry red wine

1/2 tablespoon Dijon mustard

Kosher salt and freshly ground pepper

WINE-GLAZED ROASTED WALNUTS

1 1/2 cups Merlot or other dry red wine

3/4 cup walnut halves

1/2 teaspoon kosher salt

2 teaspoons sugar

1/4 teaspoon red pepper flakes

5 ounces mixed baby salad greens

3/4 cup crumbled fresh white goat cheese

Chopped yellow and red bell peppers for garnish

TO MAKE THE DRESSING: In a small sauté pan or skillet, heat the 3 tablespoons olive oil over medium heat. Add the red onion and thyme and sauté until browned, 8 to 10 minutes. Add the wine and stir to scrape up the browned bits from the bottom of the pan. Cook to reduce slightly. Let cool, then whisk in the 1/4 cup olive oil, the mustard, and salt and pepper to taste. Refrigerate until ready to use. Whisk before serving.

TO MAKE THE WALNUTS: Add the red wine to a small stainless-steel pan and bring to a gentle boil. Reduce heat and simmer until the liquid reduces to about 1/4 cup. Be careful not to over-reduce the wine or it may burn. Transfer the pan to an ice bath and let the syrup cool.

Preheat the oven to 375°F. In a small bowl, combine the walnuts, wine syrup, salt, sugar, and red pepper flakes and mix thoroughly. Spread the walnuts onto a rimmed baking sheet and bake until nicely toasted, 10 to 12 minutes.

To serve, divide the salad greens among salad plates. Spoon the onions and dressing over the greens. Crumble the goat cheese over the onions. Garnish with the walnuts and chopped bell peppers.

~Serves 4 as a first course~

Crab, Grapefruit, and Orange Salad with Avocado Dressing

Recommended wine:
Sauvignon/Fumé Blanc

Alternative wine:
Chardonnay

The dressing for this elegant composed salad is based on a reduction of citrus juices and white wine. Sauvignon/Fumé Blanc is the preferred wine because of its general lack of oak and its exuberant fruitiness, which will amplify the dressing. The obvious choice to drink with the salad is Sauvignon/Fumé Blanc; however, the dressing will also work well with a less-oaky Chardonnay.

AVOCADO DRESSING

1 egg

2 cloves roasted garlic (see note, page 33)

1/4 cup olive oil

1/2 avocado, peeled, pitted, and sliced

1/3 cup buttermilk

2 teaspoons minced fresh tarragon, or 1 teaspoon dried tarragon

2 tablespoons white wine, preferably Sauvignon/Fumé Blanc

Juice from 1 small Valencia orange or blood orange

1 tablespoon fresh lemon juice

1 tablespoon white wine vinegar

1 tablespoon minced shallot

Kosher salt and freshly ground pepper

TO MAKE THE DRESSING: Boil the egg for 90 seconds. Transfer to cold water to cool to the touch, then peel and separate; reserve the white for another use. In a blender or food processor, combine the egg yolk and roasted garlic and process for 15 to 20 seconds. With the machine running, drizzle in the oil to make an emulsified sauce. Add the avocado, buttermilk, and tarragon and process until smooth. Transfer to a small bowl.

In a small saucepan, combine the wine, orange juice, lemon juice, vinegar, and shallot. Bring to a simmer and cook to reduce by half. Let cool, then whisk in the avocado mixture. Season with salt and pepper.

Divide the greens evenly among salad plates. Divide the crabmeat over the greens in the center of each plate. Place the grapefruit and orange slices around the salad. Spoon the dressing over the top, reserving any leftover dressing for another use. Sprinkle with pine nuts and serve.

5 ounces mixed baby greens

12 ounces fresh lump crabmeat, picked over for shell

1 large pink grapefruit, peeled and segmented (see note)

3 small navel oranges or blood oranges, peeled and segmented (see note)

2 tablespoons pine nuts, toasted, for garnish (see note, page 35)

❉ NOTE: **To peel and segment citrus,** cut a slice off the top and bottom of the citrus down to the flesh. Place the fruit on end on the cutting board and use a large, sharp knife to cut off the peel down to the flesh in long vertical pieces. Holding the fruit over a bowl, cut on either side of each membrane to release the segments.

~Serves 4 as a first course~

Chilled Fennel Soup with Anise-Flavored Shrimp

Recommended wine:
Sauvignon/Fumé Blanc

Alternative wine:
Chardonnay

This soup combines three different variations of anise—fennel, fennel seed, and Pernod—into an aromatic, flavorful soup garnished with slightly spicy shrimp. The fennel and onions are sautéed and then simmered in wine and stock. Sauvignon/Fumé Blanc, which often exhibits an aniselike note, provides the perfect counterpoint.

ANISE-FLAVORED SHRIMP

18 medium shrimp (about 12 ounces), shelled and deveined

3 tablespoons Pernod or dry white wine

2 tablespoons minced fresh mint

3 teaspoons sesame chili oil

3 teaspoons seasoned rice vinegar

1 teaspoon fennel seeds, toasted and ground

1 teaspoon minced garlic

1/4 teaspoon kosher salt

Pinch of freshly ground pepper

1/4 cup olive oil

2 pounds fennel bulbs (about 3 bulbs), cored and chopped (dark green fronds reserved)

1 1/2 large yellow onions, chopped

TO MAKE THE SHRIMP: In a medium bowl, combine all the ingredients. Cover and refrigerate for at least 30 minutes or up to 3 hours.

In a large soup pot, heat the oil over medium heat. Add the fennel, onions, garlic, thyme, and fennel seed and sauté until the fennel softens, 12 to 14 minutes. Add the wine and bring to a boil. Reduce heat and simmer for 3 to 4 minutes. Add the 6 cups stock and bring to a boil. Reduce heat to a simmer, cover, and cook for 20 minutes.

In batches, purée the soup and sour cream in a blender or food processor. Season with salt and pepper. Refrigerate until ready to serve. Thin with more stock, if necessary.

In a large sauté pan, skillet, or wok over high heat, sauté the shrimp, stirring constantly, until evenly pink, 1 to 2 minutes.

To serve, ladle the soup into 6 shallow soup bowls. Arrange 3 shrimp on the rim of each or arrange in a crisscross pattern in the center of the soup, tail ends protruding.

VARIATION: This soup may also be served warm.

~Serves 6 as a first course~

2 cloves garlic, minced

2 tablespoons minced fresh thyme, or 1 tablespoon dried thyme

2 teaspoons fennel seed, ground

1 cup dry white wine

6 cups low-salt vegetable or chicken stock, plus more as needed

1 cup sour cream

Kosher salt and freshly ground pepper

Cheese Fondue with Roasted Garlic and Sun-Dried Tomatoes

Recommended wine:
Sauvignon/Fumé Blanc

Alternative wine:
Chardonnay

I have fond memories of Sunday night dinners, enjoying one of my mother's culinary masterpieces of the sixties: cheese fondue. Runny and gooey, fondue typified "comfort food," particularly during the rainy winters. Armed with wooden skewers, we dunked San Francisco's finest sourdough into an unctuous pool of melted cheese until we were stuffed. Fondue is making a comeback, and this recipe adds roasted garlic and sun-dried tomatoes to the traditional wine-and-kirsch-based mixture. Sauvignon Blanc's tart acidity and Chardonnay's buttery texture make either wine a satisfying choice.

2 cups dry white wine

1 3/4 tablespoons cornstarch

4 cloves roasted garlic (see note, page 33), 1 whole and 3 chopped

3 cups (12 ounces) shredded Gruyère cheese

3 cups (12 ounces) shredded Emmenthal cheese

1 cup dry-packed sun-dried tomatoes, soaked in hot water for 15 minutes, drained, and julienned

3 tablespoons kirsch (see note)

1/4 teaspoon freshly grated nutmeg

1/4 teaspoon salt

1 large loaf French or Italian sourdough bread, cut into 1-inch cubes

In a medium bowl, whisk the wine and cornstarch together to dissolve the cornstarch.

Set a ceramic fondue pot on the table over a heat source and put a bread basket alongside, together with long metal fondue forks or wooden skewers. Rub the bottom of the pot with 1 roasted garlic clove. Light the burner under the fondue pot. Pour in the wine mixture and heat until almost boiling. Gradually add the cheese, stirring with a fork until melted. This will take 8 to 10 minutes. When the cheese has completely melted, stir in the remaining roasted garlic, the sun-dried tomatoes, kirsch, nutmeg, and salt.

To serve, have each guest place a piece of bread on a fork and dip the skewer into the fondue, then twirl it over the pot until it has stopped dripping. Lower the heat if the fondue begins to thicken too much.

❖ NOTE: **Kirsch** is a clear cherry brandy traditionally used to flavor fondue.

~Serves 6 to 8 as an entrée~

Shiitake Mushroom Risotto with Lemongrass and Ginger

Perfect risotto depends on a willingness to add and stir wine and stock into the rice, and the patience to keep doing so until the rice is properly al dente. This twist on the Italian classic veers into the Asian realm with a delicious punch from shiitakes, lemongrass, and ginger. It can be served as a first course, as a main course topped with grilled shrimp, or as an accompaniment to Curried Lamb Shanks (page 174) alongside a vibrant, fruity Pinot Noir or an aromatic, fruit-filled Viognier.

Recommended wine:
Pinot Noir

Alternative wine:
Viognier

4 to 5 cups low-salt chicken stock

6 tablespoons olive oil

2 tablespoons minced shallots

6 ounces sliced shiitake mushrooms, stemmed and sliced

2 tablespoons minced lemongrass or mixed grated lemon and lime zest

2 1/2 tablespoons minced fresh ginger

1 1/2 cups Arborio rice

3/4 cup dry white wine

1/4 teaspoon ground saffron threads

2 tablespoons minced fresh mint

2 tablespoons minced fresh cilantro

2 tablespoons unsalted butter at room temperature

In a medium saucepan, bring the stock to a low simmer.

In a large sauté pan or skillet, heat 4 tablespoons of the oil over medium heat. Add the shallots, mushrooms, lemongrass or zest, and ginger and sauté for 4 to 5 minutes. Add the remaining 2 tablespoons oil. Add the rice and stir until opaque. Add the wine and cook, stirring, to reduce by half. Add the stock in 1/4-cup increments, stirring constantly and cooking until each addition is absorbed. When all the stock has been added, the rice should be al dente (firm but cooked through); if not, add a little hot water and cook a little longer. Add the saffron, mint, and cilantro and stir in thoroughly. Cook for 2 to 3 minutes. Remove from heat and stir in the butter. Serve at once.

~Serves 6 as a first course or side dish, 4 as an entrée~

Pea and Leek Risotto with Basil, Tarragon, and Goat Cheese

Recommended wine:
Sauvignon/Fumé Blanc

Alternative wine:
Chardonnay

Risotto craves, in fact depends on, wine. Without wine, it's just soupy rice with no flavor foundation or perfume. The addition of wine to the sautéed rice awakens the rice and begins its swelling transformation into its succulent finished form. The herbal and vegetable notes and tart goat cheese in this risotto call for a clean, crisp, herbal-tinged Sauvignon/Fumé Blanc. This recipe was inspired by Deborah Madison, whose vegetarian cookbooks have delighted cooks everywhere.

1 cup salted water

2 cups packed fresh basil leaves

2 pounds green peas, shelled (about 2 cups)

Kosher salt and freshly ground white pepper

4 1/2 to 5 cups low-salt vegetable or chicken stock

3 tablespoons unsalted butter or olive oil, or 1 1/2 tablespoons *each*

1 leek, including light green parts, rinsed and finely diced

1/2 cup chopped yellow onion

1 tablespoon minced shallot

1 1/2 cups Arborio rice

3/4 cup dry white wine

2 tablespoons fresh white goat cheese at room temperature

2 tablespoons minced fresh tarragon

3/4 cup cherry tomatoes, hulled and halved, for garnish

In a small saucepan, bring the salted water to a boil. Add the basil and cook for 1 minute. Turn off heat and stir in 1 cup of the peas. Let stand for about 5 minutes. Drain the peas and basil and transfer to a blender or food processor. Purée until smooth. Season with salt and pepper. Set aside.

In a small saucepan, bring the stock to a low simmer. In a large, heavy saucepan, melt the butter and/or oil over medium-high heat. Add the leek and onion and sauté until the leek begins to soften, 7 to 8 minutes. Add the shallot and cook for 1 to 2 minutes. Season with salt and pepper.

Add the rice and stir until it is opaque. Add the wine and simmer, stirring, until completely absorbed. Add 2 cups of the hot stock and simmer until absorbed by the rice, stirring often. Continue to add the stock in 1/2-cup increments, stirring constantly, until each addition is absorbed. When all the stock has been added, the rice should be almost al dente (firm but cooked through).

Stir in the purée and the remaining peas. Cook and stir until the peas are just cooked through and the rice is al dente, 2 to 3 minutes. Remove from heat and stir in the goat cheese and tarragon. Taste and adjust the seasoning.

To serve, divide the risotto among warmed pasta or shallow soup bowls. Garnish the rims of the bowls with cherry tomatoes.

~Serves 4 to 6 as an appetizer, 2 to 3 as an entrée~

Beet and Syrah Risotto with Gorgonzola and Parsley-Walnut Pesto

Recommended wine:
Syrah or Shiraz

Alternative wine:
Cabernet Sauvignon

In addition to being a radiant red color, this Syrah-infused risotto oozes with flavor from the sweet roasted beets, savory leeks, and succulent Gorgonzola. This commingling of flavors is topped off with a brilliantly green parsley pesto. I serve it topped with grilled pork tenderloin or loin of venison, but it's also wonderful on its own. Accompany it with a juicy, peppery California Syrah, Australian Shiraz, or a proprietary Rhône blend featuring Syrah and other regional grapes, to echo the flavors in the risotto.

PARSLEY-WALNUT PESTO

3 tablespoons chopped walnuts, toasted (see note, page 35)

1 1/4 cups loosely packed fresh flat-leaf parsley leaves

1 tablespoon roasted garlic (see note, page 33)

1/4 cup olive oil

Kosher salt and freshly ground pepper

3 red beets, scrubbed

2 1/2 tablespoons olive oil

Kosher salt and freshly ground white pepper

3 tablespoons unsalted butter

1 cup chopped leek, rinsed

1 cup chopped yellow onions

1 large shallot, minced

TO MAKE THE PESTO: In a food processor, combine the walnuts, parsley, and roasted garlic and process until smooth. With the machine running, gradually drizzle in the oil to make an emulsified sauce. Season with salt and pepper. Transfer to a bowl, cover, and refrigerate.

Preheat the oven to 375°F. Coat the beets with 1/2 tablespoon of the olive oil and place in a roasting pan. Sprinkle with salt and pepper. Bake until tender when pierced with a knife, 45 to 50 minutes. Remove from the oven and let cool. Peel, dice, and set aside.

In a large sauté pan or skillet, melt the butter with the remaining 2 tablespoons olive oil over medium heat. Add the leek, onions, and shallot and sauté until they begin to soften, 7 to 8 minutes.

1 1/2 cups Arborio rice

1 cup Syrah or other dry red wine

4 1/2 to 5 cups low-salt vegetable or chicken stock, heated

3/4 cup crumbled Gorgonzola cheese

Diced yellow tomato or yellow bell pepper for garnish

Add the rice to the leek mixture and sauté until opaque. Add the wine and simmer, stirring constantly, until all the liquid is completely absorbed. Add 2 cups of the heated stock and simmer until the liquid is absorbed. Continue adding the stock in 1/2-cup increments and stirring until each addition is absorbed and the rice is al dente (firm but cooked through). Stir in the Gorgonzola and beets and heat through. Season with salt and pepper.

Divide the risotto among warmed pasta or shallow soup bowls. Dollop pesto on top or around the rims. Garnish with diced tomatoes or bell pepper. Serve at once.

~Serves 6 as an appetizer, 4 as an entrée~

Pan-Seared Scallops on Artichoke Purée with Grapefruit Essence

Recommended wine:
Sauvignon/Fumé Blanc

Alternative wine:
Pinot Gris/Grigio

A reduction of Sauvignon/Fumé Blanc and grapefruit juice creates a sweet-tart counterpoint to the sweetness of scallops, the grassy flavors of artichoke purée, and the heat of radishes. Serve with a tangy California or New Zealand Sauvignon/Fumé Blanc or a crisp Pinot Gris/Grigio.

12 large sea scallops (about 1 3/4 pounds total)

1 tablespoon fruity olive oil

1 teaspoon grated pink grapefruit zest

1 1/2 teaspoons chopped fresh chervil or flat-leaf parsley

Kosher salt and freshly ground white pepper

GRAPEFRUIT ESSENCE

2 tablespoons finely chopped red onion

1 cup fresh pink grapefruit juice

1/2 cup Sauvignon Blanc or Fumé Blanc wine

2 to 3 tablespoons olive oil

1/2 teaspoon Dijon mustard

Kosher salt and freshly ground black pepper

In a large bowl, combine the scallops, oil, zest, chervil or parsley, salt, and pepper. Cover and refrigerate for 1 hour or up to 2 hours.

TO MAKE THE ESSENCE: In a small saucepan, combine the onion, grapefruit juice, and wine and bring to a simmer. Cook to reduce by half. Remove from heat, strain into a small bowl, and let cool. Whisk in the oil and mustard and season with salt and pepper.

TO MAKE THE PURÉE: In a medium saucepan, combine the artichokes, stock, and chervil or parsley. Bring to a simmer and cook for 3 to 4 minutes. Transfer to a blender or food processor and purée until smooth. Return to the saucepan and add the butter and green onion. Cook over low heat to melt the butter. Set aside and keep warm.

In a lightly oiled large grill pan or skillet over medium-high heat, sear the scallops for 3 to 4 minutes on each side, or until golden brown on the outside and barely translucent in the center.

ARTICHOKE PURÉE

Two 14-ounce cans water-packed baby artichokes, rinsed, drained, and halved

1 3/4 cups low-salt chicken or vegetable stock

5 sprigs chervil or flat-leaf parsley

2 tablespoons unsalted butter

1 green onion, including light green parts, chopped

GARNISH

8 red radishes, trimmed and thinly sliced

Chervil or flat-leaf parsley sprigs

Caviar (optional)

To serve, spoon a bed of artichoke purée in the center of each warmed plate. Place a round dollop of overlapping radishes on top of the purée. Place 2 scallops on top of the radishes. Drizzle the essence over the scallops and around the edge of the plate. Garnish with herb sprigs and caviar, if desired.

~Serves 6 as a first course~

Cioppino with Mussels

Recommended wine:
Pinot Gris/Grigio

Alternative wine:
Sangiovese (Chianti Classico)

2 tablespoons olive oil

2 cups chopped yellow onions

3 cloves garlic, minced

1 green bell pepper, seeded, deribbed, and chopped

2 stalks celery, chopped

1 teaspoon dried thyme

1 teaspoon minced fresh dill

1/4 cup chopped fresh basil

2 cups dry red wine

One 28-ounce can chopped tomatoes with juice

4 1/2 cups low-salt fish or chicken stock

Cioppino, an Italian shellfish stew, is an old San Francisco tradition based on the Bay Area's famed Dungeness crab. Garlic, onions, and herbs cooked in red wine with tomatoes flavor the stew, along with fish and shellfish. Despite the red wine in the soup, a crisp, fruity Pinot Gris/Grigio is an appropriate table wine, although Chianti Classico is a good alternative pairing. If using cracked crabs, large soup bowls and a shell bowl, along with plenty of paper napkins, will be required. Serve with a warmed sourdough baguette.

In a large, heavy soup pot, heat the oil over medium heat and sauté the onions, garlic, bell pepper, and celery until the onions are soft, 6 to 8 minutes. Add the thyme, dill, and basil and sauté 2 minutes longer. Add the wine, tomatoes, stock, and bay leaf. Bring to a boil. Reduce heat to a simmer, cover, and cook for 1 1/2 hours. Add the crab, fish, and lemon juice. Put the mussels in the stew, cover, and cook until the mussels open, 3 to 5 minutes. Remove the mussels from the shell and add to the stew. Discard any mussels that don't open. Discard the bay leaf. Season with salt and red pepper flakes.

To serve, ladle into large soup bowls, making sure that the fish and shellfish are evenly divided among them. Garnish with parsley.

~Serves 4 to 6 as an entrée~

1 bay leaf

12 ounces fresh lump crabmeat, picked over for shell, or 2 cracked cooked Dungeness crabs

1 pound bass, shark, halibut, or snapper fillets, cut into small pieces

2 tablespoons fresh lemon juice

3 pounds mussels, scrubbed and debearded

Kosher salt and red pepper flakes

3 tablespoons chopped fresh flat-leaf parsley for garnish

Shrimp Cakes with Spicy Sun-Dried Tomato and Red Pepper Sauce

Recommended wine:
Champagne or sparkling wine

Alternative wine:
Viognier

These shrimp cakes have a succulent taste and a good texture since the shrimp are not too finely chopped. A spicy sauce greatly enhances their appeal. They can be served atop mixed greens or with a cream sauce. The sparkle and effervescence of Champagne or the exuberant fruit of Viognier will flatter these harmonious flavors.

3/4 teaspoon olive oil

12 ounces large shrimp, shelled and deveined

1/4 cup dry white wine

1/4 cup mayonnaise

3/4 teaspoon Dijon mustard

2 tablespoons minced fresh flat-leaf parsley

1 teaspoon minced fresh tarragon, or 1/2 teaspoon dried

1 1/4 tablespoons minced fresh chives

1/4 teaspoon Tabasco sauce

1 1/2 teaspoons balsamic vinegar

1/2 cup panko (see note) or dried bread crumbs, plus more as needed

Kosher salt and freshly ground pepper

In a medium sauté pan or skillet, heat the 3/4 teaspoon oil over medium heat. Add the shrimp and wine and cook until the shrimp are evenly pink, about 2 to 3 minutes. Using a slotted spoon, transfer the shrimp to a bowl. When cooled enough to handle, coarsely chop the shrimp. Simmer the liquid for 30 seconds to 1 minute. Remove from heat and set aside.

In a large bowl, combine the mayonnaise, mustard, parsley, tarragon, chives, Tabasco sauce, balsamic vinegar, and pan liquid and whisk thoroughly. Add the 1/2 cup panko or bread crumbs and the shrimp. Season with salt and pepper. Mix thoroughly and add more bread crumbs if needed to bind. Gently form into 4 patties. Cover and refrigerate.

TO MAKE THE SAUCE: Soak the sun-dried tomatoes in a bowl of hot water for 45 minutes. Drain and chop.

In a large sauté pan or skillet, heat the 1 tablespoon oil over medium-high heat. Add the onion, shallot, red bell pepper, and sun-dried tomatoes and sauté for 6 to 7 minutes. Add the capers, basil, cumin, adobo sauce (if using), and cayenne and cook for 2 minutes. Add the wine and 1/2 cup of the stock. Cook to reduce by half. Transfer to a blender or food processor and purée until smooth. Return to the pan and add the remaining 1/2 cup stock. Season with salt and pepper. Set and keep warm.

SPICY SUN-DRIED TOMATO AND RED PEPPER SAUCE

1 cup dry-packed sun-dried tomato halves

1 tablespoon olive oil

1/2 cup chopped yellow onion

1 tablespoon minced shallot

1 cup chopped red bell pepper

2 teaspoons capers

1 1/2 tablespoons minced fresh basil

1/2 teaspoon ground cumin

1/2 teaspoon adobo sauce (optional)

1/8 teaspoon cayenne pepper, or more to taste if not using adobo sauce

1/2 cup dry white wine

1 cup low-salt vegetable or chicken stock, or more as needed

Kosher salt and freshly ground pepper

1 tablespoon olive oil

5 ounces mixed salad greens

Flat-leaf parsley sprigs and chopped yellow bell pepper for garnish

Preheat the oven to 375°F. In a large ovenproof sauté pan or skillet, heat the 1 tablespoon oil over medium heat. Sauté the shrimp cakes until browned on one side, 4 to 5 minutes. Turn carefully and cook until browned on the second side, for 3 to 4 minutes. Put the pan in the oven and bake until heated through, 5 to 6 minutes.

To serve, divide the greens among 4 salad plates. Place a shrimp cake on top of each serving. Garnish with parsley and yellow bell pepper. Drizzle with the sauce and serve the remaining sauce alongside.

VARIATION: Add 1/2 cup heavy cream or half-and-half to the sauce along with the remaining 1/2 cup stock. Heat over low heat for 2 or 3 minutes. Set aside and keep warm while cooking the shrimp cakes. Delete the salad greens and pool the warm sauce on 4 warmed plates. Place a shrimp cake on each plate, garnish, and serve.

❖ **NOTE: Panko** are flaky Japanese bread crumbs. They're found in the Asian sections of better grocery stores and in Asian markets.

~Serves 4 as a first course~

Pepita-Crusted Salmon with Crab, Shrimp, and Vegetable Ragout

Recommended wine:
Pinot Noir

Alternative wine:
Viognier

This exciting, thoroughly New World dish is adapted from a recipe by chef Robert Kinkead of Kinkead's in Washington, D.C. Pumpkin seeds, tortilla chips, corn kernels, chilies, and tomatillos add both texture and flavor. A white wine deglazing melds all the flavors together and highlights the vegetable ragout. Heighten the effect with a fruit-forward Pinot Noir or an aromatic Viognier.

1/2 cup shelled pumpkin seeds (see note) or pistachios, lightly toasted (see note, page 35)

1/8 cup unsalted tortilla chips

1/4 teaspoon kosher salt

1/4 teaspoon red pepper flakes

6 salmon fillets (2 to 2 1/2 pounds total), pin bones and skin removed

1 cup buttermilk

CRAB, SHRIMP, AND VEGETABLE RAGOUT

2 ears corn, shucked

4 tablespoons peanut oil

1 cup chopped red onion

2 cloves garlic, minced

12 large shrimp (about 8 ounces), shelled and deveined

1/3 cup dry white wine or dry sherry

4 green onions, including light green parts, finely chopped

2 poblano chilies, roasted, peeled, and diced (see note, page 33)

In a blender or food processor, chop the pumpkin seeds, tortilla chips, salt, and red pepper flakes to a medium-coarse mixture. Dip each salmon fillet in buttermilk on one side only, then dip that side into the *pepita* mixture. Let stand for 5 minutes. Cover and refrigerate, crust-side up, for at least 45 minutes or up to 90 minutes.

TO MAKE THE RAGOUT: Blanch the corn in salted boiling water until tender, about 5 minutes. Using a large knife, cut the kernels from the cob. You should have about 1 cup. Set aside.

In a very large sauté pan or skillet, heat 2 tablespoons of the peanut oil over medium-high heat and sauté the red onion until translucent, 4 to 5 minutes. Add the garlic and sauté for 2 more minutes. Add the shrimp and sauté for 2 to 3 minutes, or until evenly pink. Add the wine and stir to scrape up the browned bits from the bottom of the pan. Add the corn, green onions, poblanos, tomatillos, potatoes, lime juice, tomatoes, cilantro, and crabmeat and sauté for 5 to 6 minutes. Stir in the butter. Season with salt and pepper. Set aside and keep warm.

Preheat the oven to 375°F. In a large ovenproof sauté pan or skillet, heat the remaining 2 tablespoons peanut oil over medium-high heat. Sauté the fillets, crust-side down, for about 5 minutes or until starting to brown. Turn the fillets over and place the pan in the oven until the salmon is almost opaque throughout, about 6 minutes.

4 tomatillos, husked, rinsed, and diced

6 small unpeeled red potatoes, boiled until tender (about 20 minutes) and diced

2 tablespoons fresh lime juice

3 plum tomatoes, seeded and diced (see note, page 68)

Leaves from 1 bunch cilantro

6 ounces fresh lump crabmeat, picked over for shell

3 tablespoons unsalted butter

Kosher salt and freshly ground pepper

GARNISH

3 plum tomatoes, seeded and diced (see note, page 68)

2 tablespoons fresh lime juice

1/4 cup fresh cilantro leaves

In a small bowl, combine all the garnish ingredients.

To serve, divide the ragout among 6 warmed plates and top each with a salmon fillet, crust-side up. Dollop with the garnish.

❊ NOTE: **Shelled pumpkin seeds, also called *pepitas*, can be found in Latino markets or the Latino sections of many supermarkets.**

~Serves 6 as an entrée~

Monkfish Tagine

Recommended wine:
Viognier

Alternative wine:
Pinot Gris/Grigio

Chef Heidi Krahling of Insalata's in San Anselmo, California, packs a lot of flavor intensity into her food, as this adapted version of one of her recipes proves. The poached monkfish recipe has the decidedly Moroccan taste of harissa. An aromatic Viognier or Pinot Gris/Grigio is an ideal choice to refresh the palate.

TAGINE BASE

4 tablespoons unsalted butter

2 cups chopped yellow onions

2 teaspoons ground turmeric

1 tablespoon ground cinnamon

3/4 tablespoon ground ginger

3/4 tablespoon sweet Hungarian paprika

2 tablespoons ground cumin

4 cloves garlic, minced

1/4 cup harissa (recipe follows)

One 28-ounce can chopped tomatoes with juice

1 1/4 cups low-salt fish stock or clam juice

1/3 cup fruity white wine

Kosher salt and freshly ground pepper

Flour for dredging

Kosher salt and freshly ground pepper

TO MAKE THE TAGINE BASE: In a medium saucepan or skillet, melt the butter over medium heat and sauté the onions until soft, about 6 minutes. Add the turmeric, cinnamon, ginger, paprika, cumin, garlic, harissa, tomatoes, stock or clam juice, and wine. Simmer for 15 minutes. Season with salt and pepper. Set aside and keep warm.

Put the flour in a shallow bowl and stir in the salt and pepper. Dredge the fish pieces in the seasoned flour to coat evenly. In a medium sauté pan or skillet, heat the oil over medium-high heat. Add the fish pieces, carrot, and zucchini and sauté until lightly browned on all sides, 4 to 5 minutes. Using a slotted spoon, transfer the fish and vegetables to the tagine base. Cover and simmer until the carrots are tender, 8 to 10 minutes.

Mound the couscous in each of 4 warmed shallow bowls. Divide the fish and vegetables evenly over the couscous. Pour the sauce over. Garnish with cilantro sprigs and serve.

~Serves 4 as an entrée~

Four 6-ounce pieces monkfish or grouper, cut into 2-inch chunks

2 tablespoons olive oil

1 carrot, peeled and cut into 1-inch-thick slices

1 zucchini, cut into 1-inch-thick slices

Steamed couscous for serving

Cilantro sprigs for garnish

HARISSA

3 red bell peppers, roasted, peeled, and chopped (see note, page 33)

2 teaspoons minced serrano chili

1 large shallot, minced

1 teaspoon ground coriander

1 teaspoon sweet Hungarian paprika

1 teaspoon caraway seeds, toasted and ground (see note, page 41)

2 tablespoons olive oil

Fresh lemon juice, kosher salt, and cayenne pepper

HARISSA

Harissa is a Tunisian chili sauce that can be purchased in many gourmet sections if you prefer not to make it from scratch.

In a blender or food processor, combine the bell peppers, chili, shallot, coriander, paprika, and caraway seeds. Purée until smooth. With the machine running, drizzle in the olive oil. Season with lemon juice, salt, and cayenne.

Refrigerate any leftover harissa for up to 1 week. Use as a condiment on grilled chicken or spicy pork kabobs.   *~Makes 1 1/2 pints~*

Vermouth-Poached Sea Bass with Orange-Jicama Salsa and Fried Capers

Recommended wine:
Semillon Chardonnay

Alternative wine:
Viognier

ORANGE-JICAMA SALSA

2 large navel oranges, peeled, sectioned, and cut into 1/2-inch dice (see note, page 93)

1/2 cup finely diced red bell pepper

1 serrano chili, seeded and minced

1 cup finely diced jicama

1 green onion, including light green parts, finely chopped

3 tablespoons minced fresh cilantro, plus 4 sprigs for garnish

Juice of 1 lime

1 avocado, peeled, pitted, and cut into 1/2-inch dice

Kosher salt and freshly ground pepper

FRIED CAPERS

1 tablespoon cornmeal

1 tablespoon all-purpose flour

1/4 cup capers, drained

1/4 cup canola oil

Australian chef Suzi McKay, with McPherson Wines and Harvest Home Country House in Avenel in Victoria, Australia, inspired this recipe for a citrus-based salsa to be served with fish. The fish is poached in a court-bouillon, which infuses the fish with flavor. The poaching liquid then becomes the basis for a tasty reduction sauce. The mild fish is accentuated by the tart, sweet tang and crunch of the salsa, the buttery texture of avocado, and the salty note of fried capers. This combination of flavors and textures is complemented by an Australian Semillon Chardonnay blend or a fruity Viognier.

TO MAKE THE SALSA: In a large bowl, combine the oranges, bell pepper, chili, jicama, green onion, cilantro, and lime juice. Stir thoroughly. Gently mix in the avocado and season with salt and pepper. Set aside.

TO MAKE THE FRIED CAPERS: In a small bowl, stir the cornmeal and flour together. Toss the capers in this mixture to coat thoroughly. Using a slotted spoon, transfer the capers to a sieve and shake to remove excess coating. In small sauté pan or skillet, heat the oil over medium-high heat. Carefully add capers so as not to splatter the oil. Fry the capers until golden, stirring occasionally, 5 to 6 minutes. Using a slotted spoon, transfer the capers to paper towels to drain.

Sprinkle the fish with salt and cayenne. In a large saucepan or skillet, combine the carrot, celery, green onion, bay leaf, thyme, stock or clam juice, and wine. Bring to a low simmer. Add the fish, cover, and poach for 6 to 7 minutes. Using a spatula or tongs, gently turn the fish and cook until opaque throughout, 6 to 7 minutes. Using a spatula, transfer the fish to a plate, cover loosely with aluminum foil, and set aside.

Cook the poaching liquid to reduce it until well flavored, 5 to 7 minutes. Remove from heat and strain. Swirl in the butter and a little lemon juice to balance the sauce.

CONTINUED

CONTINUED

Vermouth-Poached Sea Bass with Orange-Jicama Salsa and Fried Capers

(CONTINUED)

4 fillets sea bass or cod, about
2 inches thick (1 1/2 pounds total)

Kosher salt and cayenne pepper

1 large carrot, peeled and diced

1 celery stalk, diced

1 green onion, including light green
parts, finely chopped

1 bay leaf

2 sprigs thyme

1 cup low-salt fish stock or clam juice

1 1/2 cups dry vermouth or dry white
wine

2 tablespoons cold unsalted butter

Few drops of fresh lemon juice

To serve, place the fish on warmed plates. Top with a dollop of salsa. (Cover and refrigerate leftover salsa for up to 1 week; serve with grilled chicken or pork.) Drizzle the sauce over the fish. Garnish with a sprinkling of fried capers and cilantro sprigs.

~Serves 4 as an entrée~

Green Onion and Ginger Explosion Shrimp

This recipe was inspired by my late friend Barbara Tropp, whose *Modern Art of Chinese Cooking* is a contemporary bible on Chinese cooking. Her use of the word *explosion* intrigued me and created my own version of this spicy dish. Chinese rice wine contributes a distinctive Asian flavor. Fresh water chestnuts are worth looking for in Chinese markets, as they resound with flavor. The ginger flavor of this dish is nicely contrasted by an off-dry Riesling or a crisp Pinot Gris/Pinot Grigio.

Recommended wine:
Riesling

Alternative wine:
Pinot Gris/Pinot Grigio

2 tablespoons Shaoxing wine (available in Asian food sections) or dry sherry

2 tablespoons low-salt soy sauce

2 teaspoons seasoned rice vinegar

1 tablespoon sesame chili oil

2 tablespoons minced fresh ginger

4 tablespoons finely chopped green onions, including green parts

12 fresh water chestnuts, peeled and thinly sliced, or 1/2 cup thinly sliced jicama

2 tablespoons corn or peanut oil

1 pound medium shrimp, shelled and deveined, tails intact

1 cup cooked rice

In a small bowl, combine the wine, soy sauce, vinegar, and chili oil and whisk thoroughly. In a medium bowl, combine the ginger, 3 tablespoons of the green onions, and the water chestnuts or jicama.

Heat a large wok or skillet over high heat until very hot. Add the oil and allow it to sizzle. Swirl to coat the pan. Add the ginger mixture and stir-fry for about 1 1/2 minutes. Add the shrimp and stir-fry for 2 minutes, or until evenly pink. Add the wine mixture and simmer until reduced slightly, about 2 minutes. Spoon over the rice. Garnish with the remaining green onions and serve.

~Serves 4 to 6 as a first course, 2 to 3 as an entrée~

Poached Trout with Lemon Butter Sauce

Recommended wine:
Chardonnay

Alternative wine:
Sauvignon/Fumé Blanc

This elegant, classic poached trout comes from Emeril Lagasse's *Every Day's a Party*. Emeril, one of the country's most visible, passionate, and talented chefs, is also one of the most fun guys I've ever known. Here, he poaches trout in a court-bouillon of white wine, carrots, and herbs. The traditional sauce is nicely complemented by a citrus-tinged, buttery Chardonnay. Serve this with parsleyed potatoes.

COURT-BOUILLON

3 cups water

1 cup dry white wine

1/4 cup sliced carrots

1 cup sliced yellow onions

1 large sprig thyme

2 bay leaves

Juice of 1 lemon (shells reserved)

1/2 teaspoon salt

1 teaspoon freshly ground pepper

4 trout fillets (5 to 6 ounces each)

1/2 teaspoon kosher salt

TO MAKE THE COURT-BOUILLON: In a large sauté pan, skillet, or fish poacher, combine the water, wine, carrots, onions, thyme, and bay leaves. Add the lemon juice and the lemon shells. Add the salt and pepper and bring to a boil over medium-high heat. Reduce heat to a low simmer and cook for 30 minutes. Remove and discard the lemon shells. Simmer gently for 12 minutes more to reduce the liquid slightly.

Season the fillets with the salt. Add the fillets to the court-bouillon, cover, and cook until the fish flakes easily with a fork, about 10 minutes. Using a slotted metal spatula, carefully transfer the fish to a plate, cover, and keep warm.

Cook the court-bouillon over medium heat to reduce it somewhat.

LEMON BUTTER SAUCE

1/4 cup minced shallots

6 lemons, peeled and quartered

1 cup dry white wine

1/8 teaspoon salt

1/8 teaspoon cayenne pepper

1/4 cup heavy cream

3/4 cup (1 1/2 sticks) unsalted cold butter, cut into pieces

1/8 teaspoon Tabasco sauce

1/4 teaspoon Worcestershire sauce

MEANWHILE, MAKE THE SAUCE: In a small nonreactive saucepan, combine the shallots, lemons, wine, salt, and cayenne. Bring to a gentle boil over medium heat and cook to reduce to a syrup. Add the cream and cook for 2 minutes, stirring a few times, then remove from heat. Whisk in the butter, 1 tablespoon at a time, to make an emulsified sauce. Add the Tabasco and Worcestershire and whisk to blend. Strain through a fine-mesh sieve and keep warm over barely tepid water.

To serve, place a fillet on each of 4 warmed serving plates and spoon 1/4 cup of the sauce over.

~Serves 4 as an entrée~

Poached Dijon Chicken on Apple, Walnut, and Blue Cheese Salad

Recommended wine:
Riesling

Alternative wine:
Pinot Gris/Grigio

This variation on Waldorf salad features chicken simmered in a mustard-flavored poaching liquid, surrounded by sweet-tart apples, bitter walnuts, and salty blue cheese. Topping off the mélange of flavors is a sweet-sour dressing similar to Italian *agrodolce*. Wine is used both in the poaching liquid and in the dressing. Enjoy with a fruity Riesling or a crisp Pinot Gris/Grigio.

POACHING LIQUID

2 cups water

1/2 cup dry white wine

1 tablespoon Dijon mustard

1/4 cup diced celery

1 yellow onion, quartered

2 sprigs tarragon

1 bay leaf

1/2 teaspoon salt

1/2 teaspoon whole peppercorns

4 skinless, boneless chicken breast halves

DRESSING

1/4 cup honey

1/4 cup water

1/4 cup white wine vinegar

1 cup Champagne or dry white wine

1 tablespoon minced shallots

1 tablespoon minced fresh tarragon

CONTINUED

TO MAKE THE POACHING LIQUID: In a large saucepan, combine all the ingredients. Bring to a boil. Reduce heat to a low simmer and cook for 35 to 40 minutes. Add the chicken breasts, cover, and cook for 10 to 12 minutes, or until opaque throughout. Using tongs, transfer chicken to a plate and let cool. Save the liquid for another use.

TO MAKE THE DRESSING: In a small bowl, combine the honey, water, vinegar, wine, shallots, tarragon, lemon juice, and mustard and whisk thoroughly. Whisk in the olive oil. Season with salt and pepper.

To serve, divide the greens among 4 salad plates. Cut the chicken into slices. Top the greens with the sliced chicken, apples, and walnuts. Spoon the dressing over. Sprinkle with the blue cheese.

~Serves 4 as an entrée~

Poached Dijon Chicken on
Apple, Walnut, and Blue Cheese Salad (CONTINUED)

DRESSING (CONTINUED)

2 teaspoons fresh lemon juice

1 teaspoon Dijon mustard

1/4 cup olive oil

Kosher salt and freshly ground
pepper

12 ounces mixed salad greens

2 red apples, cored and thinly sliced

1/2 cup walnut halves, toasted
(see note, page 35)

3/4 cup (4 ounces) crumbled blue
cheese

Greek-Style Shrimp with Retsina and Feta

Retsina, a Greek wine flavored with pine resin, is an acquired taste. However, its vaguely turpentine flavor adds a note of complexity to some rustic Greek dishes like this one. A fruit-driven Pinot Gris/Grigio is a perfect accent to the sauce and a nice counterpoint to the shrimp and feta cheese.

Recommended wine:
Pinot Gris/Grigio

Alternative wine:
Sauvignon/Fumé Blanc

1/3 cup olive oil

1 yellow onion, finely chopped

2 large cloves garlic, minced

1/2 cup retsina or dry white wine

4 tomatoes, peeled, seeded, and chopped (see note, page 68)

2 tablespoons chopped fresh oregano or 1 tablespoon dried oregano, plus oregano sprigs for garnish

1 tablespoon minced fresh flat-leaf parsley

Kosher salt and red pepper flakes

2 pounds jumbo shrimp, shelled and deveined, tail intact

3/4 cup coarsely crumbled feta cheese

Preheat the oven to 450°F. In a medium sauté pan or skillet, heat the oil over medium heat. Add the onion and sauté until golden, 6 to 7 minutes. Add the garlic and sauté for 1 to 2 minutes. Add the wine and cook to reduce slightly. Add the tomatoes, oregano, parsley, and salt and red pepper flakes to taste. Bring to a boil, then reduce heat and simmer until the sauce thickens, 7 to 8 minutes.

Remove from heat and evenly divide the sauce among 6 ramekins. Place the shrimp on top of the tomato mixture. Sprinkle the cheese on top of the shrimp.

Bake until the cheese melts and is lightly browned, 10 to 12 minutes. Garnish with oregano sprigs and serve.

~Serves 6 as a first course~

Coq au Vin

Recommended wine:
Pinot Noir

Alternative wine:
Syrah/Shiraz

1 bottle good-quality red Burgundy or Pinot Noir

1 large carrot, peeled, chopped

1 small yellow onion, cut into eighths

1 bay leaf

Bouquet garni (3 sprigs thyme, oregano, and flat-leaf parsley, tied together in a cheesecloth square)

2 cloves garlic, chopped

8 chicken legs (joined thighs and drumsticks)

Kosher salt and freshly ground pepper

4 ounces bacon or pancetta, cut into large dice

30 pearl onions, peeled

1/4 cup brandy or Cognac

Minced zest of 1/2 orange

12 cremini or shiitake mushrooms, cut into quarters (shiitakes stemmed)

Nora Pouillon, of Nora in Washington, D.C., is a superb cook and a dedicated advocate of organic foods. Here is my adaptation of her coq au vin, which was in turn inspired by the legendary Elizabeth David. Rather than braising the chicken in wine over a long period, this recipe calls for reducing the wine to an intense liquid that becomes the sauce for the chicken. A fine Côte de Nuits, Côte de Beaune, or California Pinot Noir is the perfect match. Serve with Roasted-Garlic and Horseradish Mashed Potatoes (page 188) or pasta with olive oil.

In a medium saucepan or skillet, combine the wine, carrot, onion, bay leaf, bouquet garni, and garlic. Bring to a boil. Reduce heat to a simmer and cook to reduce by half, about 20 minutes. Strain, pressing down hard on the solids with the back of a large spoon. Discard the solids.

Season the chicken pieces with salt and pepper. In a large sauté pan or skillet over medium heat, cook the bacon or pancetta until crisp. Using a slotted spoon, transfer to paper towels to drain. Heat the fat in the pan over medium-high heat. Add the pearl onions and chicken in batches and sauté until browned on all sides. Spoon off the fat in the pan. Add the brandy or Cognac and ignite very carefully with a long match, standing back from the pan when lighting. Shake the pan until the flames die down. Stir to scrape up the browned bits from the bottom of the pan.

Add the bacon, reduced red wine, and orange zest. Cover and simmer until the chicken is tender, 25 to 30 minutes. Add the mushrooms and cook until tender, 8 to 10 minutes.

2 tablespoons unsalted butter at room temperature

2 tablespoons flour mixed with 3/4 tablespoon water

Balsamic vinegar or dry red wine as needed

Minced fresh flat-leaf parsley for garnish

In a small bowl, blend the butter and flour mixture with a fork. Add a few small pieces at a time to the pan. Bring to a gentle boil and stir until the sauce is thick and smooth, adding more of the butter mixture if needed to thicken. Add a little balsamic vinegar or red wine to enliven the dish.

To serve, evenly divide the chicken among warmed plates. Garnish with parsley.

~Serves 4 as an entrée~

Grilled Quail in Red Onion Escabeche

Recommended wine:
Viognier

Alternative wine:
Manzanillo sherry

When it comes to showcasing classic Latin American flavors, Rick Bayless of Chicago's Frontera Grill and Topolobampo is unequalled. Chef, cookbook author, TV personality, and travel guide, Bayless does it all. This is an adaptation of one of his dishes, which adds sherry to an escabeche that tops grilled quail. A fruity Viognier or a Manzanillo sherry works wonders to accentuate the spicy, sweet, and tart flavors.

3 whole cloves

1/2 teaspoon whole peppercorns

1-inch piece cinnamon stick, preferably Mexican

12 partially boned quail (about 5 ounces each)

Kosher salt

RED ONION ESCABECHE

1/3 cup extra-virgin olive oil

2 red onions, cut into 1/4-inch-thick slices

6 garlic cloves, chopped

3 bay leaves

Leaves from 6 sprigs thyme, chopped, plus sprigs for garnish

Leaves from 6 sprigs marjoram, chopped, plus sprigs for garnish

2/3 cup green olives, preferably manzanillos, pitted and halved

1/2 cup dried currants

1 1/2 cups light low-salt chicken stock

In a mortar or spice grinder, pulverize the cloves, peppercorns, and cinnamon. Set 1/4 teaspoon of the mixture aside. Use the remainder to dust over both sides of the quail, then sprinkle them with salt. Cover the quail and refrigerate for at least 1 hour or as long as overnight.

TO MAKE THE ESCABECHE: In a well-seasoned cast-iron or nonstick skillet, heat the olive oil over medium heat. Add the onions and garlic. Sauté until the onions are soft, 5 to 6 minutes. Scoop out half of the onion mixture and set aside. To the onion mixture remaining in the pan, add the 1/4 teaspoon reserved ground spices along with the bay leaves, thyme, marjoram, olives, currants, stock, sherry or wine, and vinegar. Cover and simmer over medium-low heat for 15 minutes to bring the flavors together. Taste and adjust the seasoning. Stir in the jalapeño strips and remove from heat. Let cool, then stir in the reserved onions. These will add a nice crunch to the finished dish.

Light an indirect fire in a charcoal grill or preheat a gas grill to medium-high. Remove the quail from the refrigerator 30 minutes before cooking. Lightly coat the quail with oil.

Place the birds breast-side down on the grill rack over the hot part of the grill. Cover the grill and cook for 3 minutes. Flip the quail and move to the cooler portion of the grill, with the legs toward the

CONTINUED

CONTINUED

RED ONION ESCABECHE (CONTINUED)

1/2 cup manzanillo or fino sherry or dry white wine

3 tablespoons sherry vinegar

3 large pickled jalapeño chilies, stemmed, seeded, and cut into thin lengthwise strips

Olive oil for coating

hot part. Cover and grill for 3 to 4 minutes, or until lightly pink at the bone. Don't overcook. Transfer the quail to a plate.

To serve, place 2 quail slightly overlapping on each of 6 warmed plates. Spoon a portion of escabeche over each one. Garnish with the herb sprigs.

The finished dish keeps beautifully for a couple of days. Remove from the refrigerator about 1 hour before serving to serve at room temperature, or reheat.

VARIATION: To serve at room temperature, arrange the hot grilled quail in a deep serving platter and pour all the escabeche over them. Let cool. Garnish with herb sprigs.

~Serves 12 as an appetizer, 6 as an entrée~

Rack of Lamb with Hazelnut, Roasted Garlic, and Thyme Crust and Merlot Essence

Recommended wine:
Merlot

Alternative wine:
Cabernet Sauvignon

In this recipe, adapted from one by Jimmy Schmidt of the Rattlesnake Club in Detroit, an intense essence of reduced Merlot contributes to a flavorful rack of lamb. Serve with Merlot to mirror the reduction, or with Cabernet Sauvignon for contrast. Accompany with Maytag Blue Cheese Polenta Cylinders (page 187).

MERLOT ESSENCE

1 bottle good-quality Merlot wine

1 cup low-salt lamb, veal, or chicken stock

1 tablespoon peppercorns

Kosher salt

HAZELNUT, ROASTED GARLIC, AND THYME CRUST

1/4 cup hazelnuts, toasted, skinned, and finely chopped (see note)

1/4 cup fresh bread crumbs

2 tablespoons roasted garlic (see note, page 33)

1/2 cup minced fresh chives

1/4 cup fresh thyme leaves

1/4 cup grated Parmesan cheese

Kosher salt and freshly ground pepper

About 1/4 cup Merlot wine or chicken stock, or as needed

TO MAKE THE ESSENCE: In a large saucepan, combine the Merlot, stock, and peppercorns. Bring to a boil over high heat, then reduce to a low simmer and cook until thickened enough to coat a spoon, 40 to 45 minutes. Strain through a sieve into another saucepan. Season with salt and set aside.

TO MAKE THE CRUST: In a blender or food processor, combine the hazelnuts, bread crumbs, roasted garlic, chives, and thyme, pulsing until well blended. Pulse in the Parmesan cheese. Season with salt and pepper. Drizzle in the 1/4 cup wine or stock and mix to moisten the crumbs so they will stick together; add more liquid if needed.

Preheat the broiler. Line a broiler pan with aluminum foil. Season the lamb with salt and pepper. Drizzle a little olive oil onto the lamb and coat the meat with it. Place the lamb on the prepared pan and broil about 10 inches from the heat source until well seared, about 8 minutes. Turn over and cook for 3 to 4 minutes for medium-rare. Remove from the oven and transfer to a carving board.

Bring the Merlot essence to a simmer. Brush a few tablespoons of the essence over the lamb. Pack the crust firmly onto the lamb until it adheres. Return the lamb to the broiler to lightly brown the crust, about 4 to 6 minutes. Remove from the broiler and cut into 8 double-rib chops.

1 rack of lamb (16 ribs), trimmed of fat

Kosher salt and freshly ground pepper

Olive oil for coating

Roasted-garlic olive oil and 4 sprigs thyme for garnish

To serve, cross 2 lamb chops over each other on each warmed plate. If serving with Maytag Blue Cheese Polenta Cylinders, place them in the center of the plate with the lamb chops resting against them. Drizzle the essence, then the roasted-garlic oil, artistically over the food and the plate. Garnish with a thyme sprig and serve.

✳ NOTE: **To toast and skin hazelnuts,** spread the nuts on a baking sheet and toast in a preheated 375°F oven for 5 to 8 minutes, or until browned and fragrant. Wrap the nuts in a dish towel and let cool for a few minutes. Rub the hazelnuts together inside the towel to remove the skins.

~Serves 4 as an entrée~

Smoked Pork Tenderloins with Roasted-Plum Jam

Recommended wine:
Zinfandel

Alternative wine:
Syrah/Shiraz

This recipe, adapted from one by the talented Kathy Cary of Lilly's Restaurant in Louisville, Kentucky, utilizes Zinfandel wine to roast the plums, which adds a depth of flavor to the jam. Amplify it with a vibrant berry-and-plum-tinged Zinfandel on the table. Serve with Goat Cheese and Roasted-Garlic Timbales (page 185) and minted corn.

MARINADE

2 tablespoons Dijon mustard

1 tablespoon minced fresh oregano, or 1/2 tablespoon dried oregano

1 tablespoon minced fresh thyme, or 1/2 tablespoon dried thyme

1 tablespoon fennel seed, toasted and ground (see note, page 41)

1/8 teaspoon kosher salt

1/8 teaspoon freshly ground pepper

2 pork tenderloins (about 2 1/2 pounds total)

ROASTED-PLUM JAM

10 ripe plums, pitted and halved

3 cups Zinfandel or other dry red wine

3 tablespoons maple syrup

1 tablespoon honey

2 tablespoons minced shallots

1/2 cup low-salt beef or veal stock

Kosher salt and freshly ground pepper

2 tablespoons cold unsalted butter

2 cups hickory chips

TO MAKE THE MARINADE: In a small bowl, combine all the ingredients and mix thoroughly. Rub the top and sides of the pork with the marinade. Cover and refrigerate for at least 4 hours or up to 2 days.

TO MAKE THE JAM: Preheat the oven to 350°F. Put the plums in a roasting pan, cut-side down, with 1 cup of the wine and 1 tablespoon of the maple syrup. Roast for 30 minutes. Remove from the oven and let cool. Remove the plum skins, scraping the flesh out with a sharp knife.

In a medium sauté pan or skillet, combine the remaining 2 cups wine, the remaining 2 tablespoons maple syrup, the honey, and shallots. Cook over medium heat to reduce by half. Add the stock and plum pulp. Cook to reduce by half. Season with salt and pepper. Remove from heat and stir in the butter. Set aside and keep warm.

Light an indirect fire in a charcoal grill or preheat a gas grill to low. Remove the pork from the refrigerator. Soak the hickory chips in

CONTINUED

Smoked Pork Tenderloins with Roasted-Plum Jam (CONTINUED)

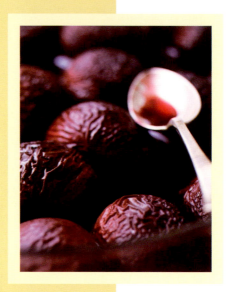

water for 30 minutes, then drain. Place a drip pan on the fuel bed, away from the hot part of the fire, and sprinkle the chips over the coals or follow the manufacturer's instructions for smoking in a gas grill. Place the tenderloins over the drip pan, cover the grill, and cook for 50 to 55 minutes, or until faintly pink in the center.

To serve, transfer the pork to a carving board and cut into slices. Overlap the slices on warmed plates and spoon the jam over.

~Serves 6 to 8 as an entrée~

Roast Veal with Fennel, Parsnips, and Sauvignon Blanc

I enjoy cooking root vegetables, such as parsnips, turnips, rutabagas, and fennel, in many different dishes. Their inimitable flavor permeates the dish with a deep, earthy sweetness. The fruit and acidity of the Sauvignon Blanc helps to balance the sweet intensity of the roasted vegetables and makes a succulent sauce. Serve this dish with wild rice mixed with sun-dried cherries.

> **Recommended wine:**
> **Sauvignon/Fumé Blanc**
>
> **Alternative wine:**
> **Chardonnay**

One 5-pound boneless shoulder or leg of veal, rolled and tied

3/4 teaspoon kosher salt

1/2 teaspoon freshly ground pepper

3/4 teaspoon sweet Hungarian paprika

1 teaspoon fennel seeds, crushed

4 tablespoons unsalted butter

1 large yellow onion, sliced

1 large leek (white part only), rinsed and chopped

3 cloves garlic, minced

1 fennel bulb, trimmed, cored, and thinly sliced

3 tablespoons minced fresh marjoram or oregano, or 1 1/2 tablespoons dried

1 bay leaf, halved

1 cup Sauvignon Blanc or other dry white wine

1 cup low-salt chicken stock

1 1/2 cups chopped fresh tomatoes

1 1/4 pounds parsnips, peeled and julienned

2 tablespoons Dijon mustard

1/2 cup minced fresh flat-leaf Italian parsley

Season the veal with the salt, pepper, paprika, and fennel seeds.

In a large Dutch oven or flameproof casserole, melt 2 tablespoons of the butter over medium heat and brown the veal on all sides. Transfer to a plate. Add the remaining 2 tablespoons butter to the pan and sauté the onion, leek, garlic, fennel, marjoram or oregano, and bay leaf until the onion is golden, 5 to 6 minutes. Add the wine and stir to scrape up the browned bits from the bottom of the pan. Cook to reduce for 4 to 5 minutes. Add the stock, tomatoes, and parsnips and simmer for 5 to 6 minutes more.

Preheat the oven to 325°F. Place the veal on top of the vegetables and smear 1 tablespoon of the mustard over the top and sides. Put the pan in the oven and roast for 2 hours, or until an instant-read thermometer inserted in the center registers 165°F. Baste occasionally with the pan liquid.

Remove from the oven and transfer the veal to a platter. Transfer the pan with the vegetables to the stove top, stir in the remaining 1 tablespoon mustard, and bring to a simmer. Remove from heat, cover, and keep warm.

To serve, carve the veal into slices and place on warmed plates. Using a slotted spoon, place portions of the vegetables onto plates. Spoon the sauce over the veal. Sprinkle with the parsley.

~Serves 4 as an entrée~

Marinating

Of all the cooking methods that use wine, marinating is probably the one most commonly utilized by contemporary cooks. In conjunction with grilling, it borders on an American obsession. From Mediterranean combinations of red wine, garlic, and aromatic Provençal herbs to Asian ones of sake or mirin, soy, and ginger, marinades come in a dizzying array of styles. They are easy to prepare, packed with taste, beguilingly fragrant, and they help—at least with meats—to tenderize and flavor the food.

Tender cuts of meat, such as filet mignon, New York steak, and rib-eye steak, don't require tenderizing, though a marinade may be used to flavor the meat. Less tender cuts, however, such as skirt, flank, porterhouse, and tri-tip, benefit tremendously from several hours in a savory marinade.

Wine can be the unifying thread in a marinade, adding flavor of its own and providing an acidic boost to the tenderizing process. Marinades also help to extract flavors from fresh herbs, spices, and vegetables, such as onions, carrots, and celery.

Many chefs, such as the legendary Thomas Keller at the French Laundry in California's wine country, have a completely different approach to this commonly practiced technique. Keller is one who believes that marinades do not really tenderize meat; they only "cook" the surface.

After marinating meats for some time, Keller strains the marinade and then simmers it to reduce the liquid, to eliminate the alcohol, and to intensify the flavors. The reduction becomes the basis for a sauce, utilizing fresh herbs and stock, and is often finished with a little butter.

A marinade can also be reduced to a glaze and then painted onto the meat. Reduced marinades may require the addition of a little sugar or honey to balance their acidity.

Marinades can play an important role with vegetables and fruits as well. Marinating fruits such as cherries or berries is referred to as *maceration*.

MARINATING

TIPS ON MARINATING WITH WINE

:: Never use wine-based marinades in a metal container, as the acid can react with the metal. Use glass or ceramic baking dishes, or self-sealing plastic bags.

:: If placing the marinade and food in a baking dish, turn the food frequently while marinating. If using a self-sealing plastic bag, put the marinade and food to be marinated in the bag and set the bag in a baking dish in the refrigerator. Turn the bag frequently to coat all sides of the food with the marinade.

:: The larger the piece of meat and the tougher the cut, the more time it needs to marinate, from several hours to overnight, always refrigerated. Cut small slits into the surface of tougher and larger cuts to help the marinade penetrate them.

:: Meats and chicken can be marinated at room temperature or in the refrigerator for up to 2 hours. Remove refrigerated foods from the refrigerator 30 minutes before cooking.

:: Don't marinate fish and shellfish for more than $1\frac{1}{2}$ hours, or the acidity in wine will "cook" the flesh and turn it opaque.

:: If cooking a wine-based marinade before using it, make sure to let it cool so that it doesn't begin to prematurely cook the meat.

:: Adding oil to marinades allows them to be used as a basting liquid for foods, adding flavor and keeping the food from drying out.

:: Marinades to be used for basting or for sauces should be boiled for 5 minutes first to prevent bacterial contamination.

Tequila and Sherry–Marinated Prawns Diablo with Kumquats

The flavors in this marinade infuse the prawns with sweet citrus flavors and captivating heat. I prefer kumquats to Mandarin oranges, if they're available. The addition of tequila and sherry—interesting bedfellows—adds a nutty, peppery top note. A dry fino sherry is the ideal wine for sipping, as it mirrors the recipe, while a crisp, clean Italian Pinot Grigio is a suitable alternative.

Recommended wine:
Fino sherry

Alternative wine:
Pinot Grigio

1 pound jumbo prawns, shelled and deveined

2 tablespoons tequila

2 tablespoons fino sherry

2 tablespoons herb-flavored or regular olive oil

3/4 teaspoon Thai fish sauce, or 1/4 teaspoon salt

1 cup sliced kumquats, or 4 seedless Mandarin oranges, peeled and sectioned

1 teaspoon green peppercorns, drained and chopped

2 cloves garlic, chopped

2 tablespoons finely chopped green onion, including green parts

1/4 to 1/2 teaspoon red pepper flakes (to taste)

2 tablespoons minced fresh cilantro

4 butter lettuce leaves

Cilantro sprigs, chopped red and yellow bell peppers, and diced toasted almonds for garnish

In a small bowl, combine the prawns, tequila, sherry, oil, fish sauce or salt, kumquats or oranges, peppercorns, garlic, green onion, red pepper flakes, and cilantro. Refrigerate for at least 1 hour or up to 2 hours. Remove the prawns from the refrigerator 30 minutes before cooking.

Heat a large sauté pan, skillet, or wok over medium-high heat. Add the prawn mixture and sauté, stirring often, until the prawns are evenly pink, about 3 minutes.

Divide immediately among the butter lettuce leaves. Garnish with cilantro sprigs, chopped bell peppers, and a sprinkling of almonds. Serve at once.

~Serves 4 as an appetizer~

Grilled-Vegetable Escalivada with Marinated and Grilled Ahi

Recommended wine:
Tempranillo (Spanish Rioja)

Alternative wine:
Pinot Noir

While traveling in Spain in 1997, my family and I experienced a glorious *escalivada* on the Costa Brava in the little town of Lloret del Mare. This classic Spanish dish features grilled eggplant, onions, bell peppers, and tomatoes. Here, the concoction is served with grilled ahi and served at room temperature—ideal for summer alfresco dining. Either a vibrantly fruity, spicy Spanish Rioja or an earthy, fruity Pinot Noir will complement this robust, rustic dish.

MARINADE

3 tablespoons white wine vinegar

1/2 cup sherry wine vinegar

1/2 cup dry white wine

4 teaspoons olive oil

3/4 teaspoon honey

1 teaspoon cumin seeds, toasted and ground (see note, page 41)

2 teaspoons grated orange zest

1 teaspoon mixed peppercorns

1 shallot, sliced

1 teaspoon kosher salt

1 bay leaf, crumbled

2 pounds ahi tuna fillets

TO MAKE THE MARINADE: In a small bowl, combine all the ingredients. Pour into a glass or ceramic baking dish and add the tuna. Place in the refrigerator. (The tuna will turn color due to its being altered by the acidic ingredients.)

Light a fire in a charcoal grill or preheat a gas grill to high. Remove the tuna from the refrigerator 30 minutes before cooking.

TO MAKE THE *ESCALIVADA*: Place the eggplants, onions, tomatoes, and bell peppers on the grill and cook until well charred, about 25 minutes, gently turning several times with tongs. (Use care in turning the tomatoes and onions in particular.) Remove the eggplant and continue cooking the other vegetables for 6 to 7 minutes. Transfer to a platter.

Put the bell peppers in a large paper bag, close, and let cool for 15 minutes. Remove from the bag, peel and seed the peppers, and cut them into long strips. Cut the eggplant into cubes and scoop away from the charred skin. Discard the skin. Peel, seed, drain, and chop the tomatoes. Slice the onions.

In a large bowl, combine all the grilled vegetables, the roasted garlic, oil, vinegar, cumin, and paprika. Gently mix. Season with salt and pepper.

GRILLED-VEGETABLE ESCALIVADA

8 Japanese eggplants, or 3 globe eggplants, pricked with a fork

2 red onions, halved

2 1/4 pounds ripe tomatoes

2 large red bell peppers

1 tablespoon roasted garlic (see note, page 33)

2 tablespoons olive oil

1 3/4 tablespoons sherry wine vinegar

1/2 teaspoon ground cumin

1/4 teaspoon sweet Hungarian paprika

Kosher salt and freshly ground pepper

1 tablespoon chopped green onion leaves for garnish

Remove the tuna from the marinade and grill over high heat for 2 to 3 minutes on each side for rare.

To serve, spoon the *escalivada* onto plates. Slice the tuna thinly and place the slices leaning slightly against the *escalivada*. Sprinkle the green onion on top.

~Serves 4 as an entrée~

Grilled Swordfish with Roasted Red Pepper and Macadamia Pesto

Recommended wine:
Riesling

Alternative wine:
Sauvignon/Fumé Blanc

This simple marinade for fish relies on an off-dry, fruity Riesling. The vivid pesto works seamlessly with a fruity Riesling or a Sauvignon/Fumé Blanc. Serve with grilled yellow squash and zucchini as a colorful, flavorful side dish.

1 cup Riesling or other fruity white wine

6 tablespoons minced fresh cilantro

2 large shallots, minced

4 teaspoons Thai fish sauce or soy sauce

Freshly ground pepper

6 swordfish steaks (about 3 1/2 pounds total)

ROASTED RED PEPPER AND MACADAMIA PESTO

3 red bell peppers, roasted and peeled (see note, page 33)

1/3 cup macadamia nuts

2 tablespoons minced fresh cilantro, plus cilantro sprigs for garnish

2 tablespoons minced fresh ginger

2 tablespoons minced shallots

1/4 cup grated Parmesan cheese

1 or 2 chipotles en adobo (to taste), drained and chopped

3 tablespoons extra-virgin olive oil

1/2 tablespoon fresh lemon juice

Kosher salt and red pepper flakes

In a large glass or ceramic baking dish, combine the wine, cilantro, shallots, fish sauce, and pepper to taste. Add the fish, cover, and refrigerate for at least 1 hour or up to 2 hours, turning the fish occasionally.

TO MAKE THE PESTO: In a blender or food processor, combine the bell peppers, nuts, minced cilantro, ginger, shallots, and cheese. Add 1 chipotle and purée, then taste for the desired heat level before adding the second. With the machine running, gradually drizzle in the olive oil and lemon juice to make an emulsified sauce. Season with salt and red pepper flakes.

Light a fire in a charcoal grill or preheat a gas grill to high. (You can also use an oiled grill pan heated over high heat.) Remove the fish from the refrigerator 30 minutes before grilling.

Brush the grill grids with oil. Remove the swordfish from the marinade and grill for 7 to 8 minutes, or until grill-marked on the bottom. Turn and grill on the second side for 5 to 6 minutes, or until opaque throughout. Do not overcook.

To serve, place a swordfish steak on each of 6 warmed plates and dollop pesto over one edge of the steak. Garnish with cilantro sprigs.

~Serves 6 as an entrée~

Caper and Olive–Encrusted Petrale Sole with Verjus and Lemon

One of the most glorious experiences of my life was eating at the Michelin three-star Don Alfonso 1890 in Italy. At this magnificent restaurant on the tip of the Amalfi Coast, in the tiny village of Sant'Agata sui Due Golfi, Livia and Alfonso Iaccarino serve ethereal food. This simple dish, adapted from one of theirs, uses verjus, a green grape juice that contributes a tart flavor to the marinade. Enjoy with a crisp Italian white or a Sauvignon/Fumé Blanc. Serve with oven-roasted potatoes and Parmesan-topped tomato halves.

Recommended wine:
Italian Pinot Grigio or Greco di Tufo

Alternative wine:
Sauvignon/Fumé Blanc

1 1/2 pounds petrale sole fillets

Extra-virgin olive oil for drizzling

2 teaspoons pine nuts, toasted and chopped (see note, page 35)

2 tablespoons minced fresh flat-leaf parsley, plus parsley sprigs for garnish

1 1/2 tablespoons capers, drained, patted dry, and chopped

3 tablespoons dried bread crumbs

1/4 cup chopped pitted brine-cured black olives

4 teaspoons fresh lemon juice, plus thin lemon slices for garnish

4 teaspoons verjus or dry white wine

Preheat the broiler. Place the fillets on a broiler pan lined with aluminum foil. Drizzle the fish with olive oil. In a small bowl, mix the pine nuts, minced parsley, capers, and bread crumbs. Sprinkle evenly over the sole. Sprinkle the olives evenly on top. Mix the lemon juice and verjus together and drizzle over the top.

Place the pan under the broiler about 9 inches from the heat source and cook the fish until opaque throughout, 5 or 6 minutes. Remove from the oven and transfer to warmed plates. Garnish with parsley sprigs and lemon slices.

~Serves 4 as an entrée~

Grilled Salmon Fillets with Tomato and Roasted-Garlic Salsa

Recommended wine:
Riesling

Alternative wine:
Chardonnay

This pretty salmon dish relies on a good Spanish cream sherry to add a pleasing note of sweetness to the marinade. The sherry is echoed a second time in the tomato salsa. The slight sweetness of the dish calls for a fruity, off-dry Riesling, but a lightly oaked Chardonnay will also pair well. Serve this with green beans with toasted almonds.

MARINADE

2 tablespoons finely chopped yellow onion

2 tablespoons finely chopped green onion

1/4 cup Spanish cream sherry

1 tablespoon Spanish sherry vinegar

1 tablespoon olive oil

2 tablespoons minced fresh basil

Kosher salt and freshly ground pepper

2 salmon fillets (1 1/4 pounds total), pin bones removed

TO MAKE THE MARINADE: In a small bowl, combine all the ingredients and whisk thoroughly. Put the salmon in a glass or ceramic baking dish and pour the marinade over. Cover and refrigerate for at least 1 hour or up to 2 hours.

TO MAKE THE SALSA: In a medium bowl, combine all the ingredients and mix thoroughly. Cover and refrigerate for at least 1 hour or up to 2 hours.

Light a fire in a charcoal grill or preheat a gas grill to medium-high. Remove the salmon from the refrigerator 30 minutes before cooking.

Remove the salmon from the marinade and pat dry. Place the salmon on the grill, skin-side down. Cook for 6 to 7 minutes. Turn carefully, keeping the skin intact. Cook until browned on the outside and barely translucent in the center, 4 to 5 minutes.

To serve, place the salmon on warmed plates. Spoon the lightly chilled salsa on top and alongside the salmon.

~Serves 2 as an entrée~

TOMATO AND ROASTED-GARLIC SALSA

1 pound golden or red tomatoes, seeded, chopped, and drained (see note, page 68)

1 cup cherry tomatoes, halved and drained

2 tablespoons minced fresh basil

2 tablespoons finely chopped green onion

1 tablespoon minced shallots

2 cloves garlic, roasted, peeled, and chopped (see note, page 33)

1 serrano chili, seeded and minced

1 tablespoon Spanish cream sherry

1 tablespoon olive oil

1 teaspoon white wine vinegar

Kosher salt and freshly ground pepper

Grilled Asian-Style Cornish Hens with Spicy Corn Relish

Recommended wine:
Sauvignon/Fumé Blanc

Alternative wine:
Pinot Gris/Grigio

Cornish hens are juicy, tasty little birds that are perfect for the grill. This marinade adds Asian flavors to the skin and meat as they caramelize. A fruity California Sauvignon Blanc or Italian Pinot Gris/Grigio is a sublime partner to the corn and pepper relish. Serve this with grilled asparagus.

MARINADE

3/4 cup sake

2 tablespoons seasoned rice vinegar

1 1/2 tablespoons sesame chili oil

1 teaspoon white wine Worcestershire sauce or regular Worcestershire sauce

1/4 cup loosely packed fresh cilantro leaves

1 shallot, minced

1 green onion, including green parts, finely chopped

1 1/2 teaspoons Thai fish sauce

1 teaspoon ground ginger

4 Cornish hens, rinsed, patted dry, and halved

SPICY CORN RELISH

1 cup corn kernels (2 ears)

1 green onion, including light green parts, finely chopped

1 tablespoon chopped pickled ginger

TO MAKE THE MARINADE: In a small bowl, combine all the ingredients and whisk thoroughly. Place the halved hens in a large glass or ceramic baking dish and pour the marinade over. Cover and refrigerate for at least 2 hours or up to 3 hours.

TO MAKE THE RELISH: In a medium bowl, combine all the ingredients and stir to blend. Cover and refrigerate for 1 to 2 hours.

Light an indirect fire in a charcoal grill or preheat a gas grill to medium. Place the hens over the cool part of the fire, cover the grill, and cook for 15 minutes. Baste, turn, cover again, and grill for 18 to 20 minutes on the second side, or until golden brown on the outside and opaque throughout.

Place 2 hen halves on each warmed plate and spoon the relish alongside.

~Serves 4 as an entrée~

CONTINUED

Grilled Asian-Style Cornish
Hens with Spicy Corn Relish

(CONTINUED)

SPICY CORN RELISH (CONTINUED)

1/2 cup diced roasted red bell pepper
(see note, page 33)

1 chipotle chili, minced

3 tablespoons minced fresh cilantro

1 tablespoon seasoned rice vinegar

1 tablespoon herb-flavored or regular
olive oil

1 tablespoon sake

Smoked Sea Scallops in Riesling "Martinis"

This slightly frivolous but tasty recipe uses wine to poach and brine scallops, which are served with a fresh salsa in martini glasses, swimming in a mixture of fresh stock and wine. An off-dry Alsatian, German, or California Riesling is important in this dish as it provides a slightly sweet counterpoint to the smokiness of the scallops and to the heat of the chilies.

Recommended wine:
Riesling

Alternative wine:
Gewürztraminer

1 1/2 cups Riesling or other fruity white wine

2/3 cup low-salt fish stock

1 tablespoon minced shallots

8 ounces sea scallops

2 tablespoons kosher salt

2 tablespoons packed brown sugar

1 1/2 cups alder or apple wood chips

1 tablespoon diced cucumber

1 1/2 teaspoons minced serrano or jalapeño chilies

1 1/2 teaspoons diced red bell pepper

2 teaspoons finely chopped green onion

2 tablespoons diced tomato

Spanish green olives on swizzle sticks and cilantro sprigs for garnish

In a medium sauté pan or skillet, bring 1 cup of the wine, 1/3 cup of the fish stock, and the shallots to a boil. Add the scallops, reduce heat to a low simmer, cover, and poach for 2 to 3 minutes, turning once. Remove the scallops with tongs and let cool. Pour the liquid into a large nonmetal bowl and add the salt and brown sugar. Stir thoroughly to dissolve. Let cool and refrigerate.

Cut the scallops in half horizontally. Add to the brine and refrigerate for 2 hours to chill. Remove and pat dry. Discard the brine.

Soak the wood chips in water for 30 minutes. Drain. Put the wood chips in an electric smoker or in the bottom of a wok over medium-high heat. Place the scallops on the rack in the smoker or on a wire rack set in the wok. Close the smoker or cover the wok. Smoke the scallops for about 1 1/2 hours.

To serve, divide the scallops among martini glasses or shallow Champagne glasses. In a small bowl, combine the cucumber, chilies, red bell pepper, green onion, and tomato. Add the salsa to the glasses. Divide the remaining 1/3 cup fish stock and 1/2 cup wine among the glasses. Stir gently. Garnish each serving with a green olive on a swizzle stick and a sprig of cilantro hanging over the side. Accompany with spoons. Cheers!

~Serves 2 as a first course~

Grilled Veal Chops with Pancetta and Porcini in Chianti Sauce

Recommended wine:
Sangiovese (Chianti Classico)

Alternative wine:
Zinfandel

Racy, vibrant Chianti Classico, made principally from the Sangiovese grape, provides a bracing backdrop for both the marinade and sauce for this dish. The high acidity of the Sangiovese is complemented by the earthiness of the porcini and the pancetta in the sauce. A little wine is added at the very end of the reduction for brightness. Serve with roasted Yukon Gold potato wedges and summer squash.

1/4 ounce dried porcini mushrooms

MARINADE

1/3 cup chopped yellow onion

1/4 cup dry red wine, preferably Chianti Classico or Sangiovese

2 tablespoons roasted-garlic olive oil or regular olive oil

1 tablespoon balsamic vinegar

2 teaspoons minced fresh oregano, or 1 teaspoon dried oregano

1 1/2 teaspoons minced fresh tarragon, or 3/4 teaspoon dried tarragon

Kosher salt and freshly ground pepper

2 veal rib chops (about 1 1/2 pounds total)

In a small bowl, soak the porcini mushrooms in hot water for 2 hours.

TO MAKE THE MARINADE: In a medium bowl, combine all the ingredients and mix thoroughly. Put veal chops in a glass or ceramic baking dish and pour the marinade over. Cover and refrigerate for at least 2 hours or up to 3 hours.

Light a fire in a charcoal grill or preheat a gas grill to high. Remove the chops from the refrigerator 30 minutes before cooking.

MEANWHILE, MAKE THE SAUCE: In a medium saucepan or skillet, heat the oil over medium-high heat. Add the pancetta and sauté for 6 to 7 minutes, or until crisp. Add the onion, leek, and tomatoes and sauté for 4 to 5 minutes, or until the onion is soft. Add 3/4 cup of the wine. Bring to a boil, reduce heat, and cook to reduce the liquid by half. Add the stock and cook to reduce to a saucelike consistency. Add the remaining 1/4 cup wine and stir well. Remove from heat and stir in the butter. Season with salt and pepper. Set aside and keep warm.

CHIANTI SAUCE

1 tablespoon roasted-garlic olive oil or regular olive oil

3 ounces pancetta, chopped

1/3 cup chopped yellow onion

1 leek (white part only), thinly sliced, rinsed, and chopped

1 cup chopped seeded tomatoes (see note, page 68)

1 cup dry red wine, preferably Sangiovese or Chianti Classico

2 cups low-salt beef, veal, or chicken stock

2 tablespoons cold unsalted butter

Kosher salt and freshly ground pepper

Flat-leaf parsley sprigs for garnish

Remove the veal chops from the marinade and pat dry. Grill on one side for 9 to 10 minutes. Turn and cook on the second side for 6 to 7 minutes for medium-rare.

To serve, pool the sauce on warmed plates. Place a veal chop on top. Sprinkle with parsley.

~Serves 2 as an entrée~

Grilled Leg of Lamb with Feta-Mint Butter and Sun-Dried Tomato and Roasted Red Pepper Sauce

Recommended wine:
Syrah/Shiraz or a Rhône-style blend featuring Syrah

Alternative wine:
Zinfandel

A decidedly Mediterranean flavor permeates this complex dish. The lamb is marinated in red wine, while two sauces commingle in the finished preparation. A smooth, juicy Syrah/Shiraz or Rhône blend (as listed on back label) or a robust Zinfandel is a good match for the heady flavors of this dish. Serve buttered peas and orzo with lemon zest alongside.

MARINADE

1/4 cup olive oil

1 tablespoon balsamic vinegar

1 tablespoon Dijon mustard

1 bay leaf, crumbled

3/4 teaspoon hot paprika

1/4 cup chopped fresh mint leaves

1 large clove garlic, thinly sliced

1/2 cup dry red wine

1/8 teaspoon freshly ground pepper

1/4 teaspoon kosher salt

1 tablespoon herbes de Provence or dried rosemary

One 6- to 7-pound leg of lamb, boned, butterflied, and trimmed of excess fat

TO MAKE THE MARINADE: In a small bowl, combine all the ingredients and whisk thoroughly. Pour the marinade into a large self-sealing plastic bag. Add the lamb. Refrigerate for at least 3 or up to 4 hours, turning occasionally.

Light a fire in a charcoal grill or preheat a gas grill to high. Remove the lamb from the refrigerator 30 minutes before cooking.

MEANWHILE, MAKE THE BUTTER: In a blender or food processor, combine the feta, green onion, mint, vinegar, and pepper. Process until smooth. Add the pine nuts and pulse 10 to 12 times. Transfer to a small bowl. Set aside.

TO MAKE THE SAUCE: In a small saucepan, simmer the wine to reduce by half.

In a blender or food processor, combine the bell peppers, sun-dried tomatoes and oil, shallots, parsley, Tabasco, reduced wine, and vinegar. Process until smooth. Transfer to a small nonmetal bowl. Season with salt. Set aside.

CONTINUED

CONTINUED

Grilled Leg of Lamb with Feta-Mint Butter and Sun-Dried Tomato and Roasted Red Pepper Sauce (CONTINUED)

FETA-MINT BUTTER

12 ounces feta cheese, cut into chunks

1 green onion, including light green parts, finely chopped

1/3 cup minced fresh mint

1 tablespoon white wine vinegar

Pinch of freshly ground white pepper

1/4 cup pine nuts, toasted (see note, page 35)

SUN-DRIED TOMATO AND ROASTED RED PEPPER SAUCE

1/4 cup dry red wine

3 red bell peppers, roasted and peeled (see note, page 33)

One 8-ounce jar oil-packed sun-dried tomatoes

2 tablespoons minced shallots

1/3 cup minced fresh flat-leaf parsley

1/2 teaspoon Tabasco sauce

2 tablespoons red wine vinegar

Kosher salt

6 mint sprigs for garnish

Remove lamb from the marinade and pat dry. Cut the lamb into sections with approximately the same thickness. Grill for 10 to 12 minutes on one side. Turn and grill for 8 to 10 minutes, depending on thickness, for medium-rare.

To serve, cut the lamb into serving slices. Place on warmed plates and dollop with the tomato-pepper sauce. Top with feta-mint butter.

~Serves 6 as an entrée~

Braised Rabbit with Aged Balsamic Vinegar

This version of a recipe by Peter Chastain, the chef at Prima in Walnut Creek, California, adds wine to a marinade and then uses it to braise the rabbit. The flavors are accentuated by a final splash of aged balsamic vinegar, which gives the dish an intense top note. Accompany with an earthy, fruity Chianti Classico or Sangiovese or a rich Italian Barolo or Barbaresco. Serve with Maytag Blue Cheese Polenta Cylinders (page 187) and sautéed chard.

Recommended wine:
Sangiovese (Chianti Classico)

Alternative wine:
Nebbiolo (Barolo or Barbaresco)

2 rabbits, cut into loin and leg-thigh pieces

1 bottle dry white wine

3 tablespoons white wine vinegar

Leaves from 1 bunch sage, minced

Leaves from 3 sprigs rosemary, minced

1/2 bunch flat-leaf parsley, stemmed and minced, plus sprigs for garnish

4 cloves garlic, minced

1 tablespoon extra-virgin olive oil, plus 1/4 cup

Kosher salt and freshly ground pepper

2 tablespoons tomato paste

4 cups low-salt chicken or beef stock

1 teaspoon cornstarch mixed with 1 teaspoon cold water (optional)

3 tablespoons aged balsamic vinegar

Place the rabbit in a glass or ceramic baking dish and pour over 2 cups of the white wine and the vinegar. Cover and refrigerate for at least 3 hours or up to 12 hours. Remove the rabbit from the refrigerator 30 minutes before cooking.

In a mortar or a food processor, combine the sage, rosemary, the 1/2 bunch parsley, the garlic, and the 1 tablespoon olive oil and grind them to a paste.

Preheat the oven to 350°F. Remove the rabbit from the marinade and reserve the marinade. Pat the rabbit dry and season with salt and pepper. In a Dutch oven or large flameproof casserole, heat the 1/4 cup oil over medium-high heat and brown the rabbit on all sides in batches. Add the herb paste to the pan and stir until aromatic, 3 to 4 minutes. Add the reserved marinade and simmer for 15 minutes. Remove the rabbit from the pan.

Add the tomato paste to the pan and stir to blend. Add the stock and bring to a boil. Return the rabbit to the pan. Cover and bake until fork-tender, 25 to 30 minutes. Transfer the rabbit to a platter and cover loosely with aluminum foil. Return the pan to the stove and cook to reduce the pan liquid until thickened. Add the cornstarch mixture to thicken further, if you like.

To serve, divide the rabbit pieces among warmed plates and pour the sauce over. Drizzle with balsamic vinegar.

~Serves 4 as an entrée~

Braising

Braising is one of the best ways to use wine in cooking. The smell of a deeply flavored braised meat or poultry stew is enough to send diners into a state of rapture, so intense are the aromas that develop.

Braising almost always involves browning the meat in butter or oil. Browning the meat seals in the juices, creates a caramelized exterior, and adds to the color of the pan liquid when wine is added. The meat may be dusted with flour and/or herbs and spices. Liquid is then added and the pot is covered and placed in a preheated 300° to 350°F oven or cooked over low heat on the stove top for a long period of time. Depending on the recipe and kind of meat, it is not uncommon to braise dishes for 2 to 3 hours.

Less-tender cuts of meats—such as shoulder cuts, shanks, short ribs, rump, chuck, legs, and thighs—are commonly braised, since the longer cooking times and lower temperatures help to tenderize them and infuse them with flavor. During the braise, the meat slowly releases its juices into the cooking liquid and adds immeasurably to its flavor. During cooking, juices and moisture accumulate on the inside of the lid and drip down into the food to baste it.

Wine can play a prominent role in braises, contributing its incomparable ripe fruit flavors, while its acidity and tannin help to break down muscle fibers and penetrate the meat. When used in a braising liquid with wine, herbs, spices, and the entire allium family—principally onions, garlic, and shallots—add their unmistakable intensity.

Vegetables such as celery, tomatoes, and root vegetables are also often added to braises as flavorings or as an integral part of the dish.

In order to intensify the braising liquid, many cooks remove the cooked meat and vegetables from the liquid and cook the liquid to reduce it. The meat and vegetables are then returned to the liquid, which can also be finished with a mixture of cornstarch or arrowroot and water to thicken it slightly, or with butter to add a silken richness to the dish.

Braises take on many different flavors and textures, depending on their country of origin and the personal imprint of the cook. A French braise, typically involving wine, differs dramatically from a German, Italian, Caribbean, or Spanish one in which cider, rum, beer, fortified wines, or other spirits are used.

BRAISING

RECOMMENDED WINES FOR BRAISING

WINE	FOOD
Sauvignon Blanc/Fumé Blanc	Poultry, veal, vegetables
Pinot Gris/Pinot Grigio	Poultry, veal, vegetables
Chardonnay	Poultry, veal, pork, rabbit
Riesling	Poultry, veal, pork, rabbit
Cabernet Sauvignon	Beef, lamb, duck, venison
Merlot	Beef, lamb, pork, duck
Syrah/Shiraz	Beef, lamb, pork, venison
Zinfandel	Beef, lamb, pork, venison
Pinot Noir	Poultry, pork, veal

TIPS ON BRAISING WITH WINE

:: Use Dutch ovens or heavy flameproof casseroles large enough to allow some space around the meat.

:: Prior to browning, make sure that the meat is dry and at room temperature and that the pan and fat are hot.

:: When adding wine to a hot pan, stand away from it so that the steam that's released does not burn you.

:: As a general rule, use about $1/2$ cup wine for every pound of meat.

:: Use robust red wines, such as Cabernet Sauvignon, Merlot, Syrah/Shiraz, and Zinfandel, with red meats and game meats, and fruity, lower-oaked white wines, such as Chardonnay, Pinot Gris/Pinot Grigio, and Sauvignon/Fumé Blanc, with poultry, veal, pork, and game birds.

:: Aromatic herbs or spices can be added to the wine if greater intensity or more complex flavors are desired.

:: For cooking, use a wine from the same grape as the wine you'll serve with the finished dish. Although the braising wine need not be as high quality as the table wine, all wine used in cooking should be good enough to drink.

:: Virtually all braised dishes benefit from being cooked in advance and refrigerated overnight to allow the flavors to mellow. Skim the fat off the top before reheating.

Merlot-Braised Peasant Chicken with Rigatoni

Recommended wine:
Merlot

Alternative wine:
Pinot Noir

In this rustic recipe, Merlot flavors the braising liquid for the tender chicken. Served atop buttered rigatoni, it is a soul-satisfying cold-weather dish. A Merlot served at the table will add immeasurably to the pleasure. A lighter Pinot Noir is a reasonable alternative.

6 large chicken leg-thigh pieces (3 to 3 1/2 pounds total)

1/3 teaspoon kosher salt

1/4 teaspoon freshly ground pepper

2 tablespoons olive oil

1 1/4 cups sliced yellow onions

3 large cloves garlic, minced

1/2 cup diced carrots

1/2 cup chopped fennel

2 tablespoons minced fennel fronds

1 1/2 cups Merlot wine

One 14-ounce can chopped tomatoes with juice

2 tablespoons tomato paste

1/4 teaspoon red pepper flakes

1 tablespoon minced fresh basil, or 1/2 tablespoon dried basil

Remove the skin from the chicken. Season the chicken with salt and pepper. In a large Dutch oven or flameproof casserole, heat the olive oil over medium-high heat and cook the chicken until browned, about 4 to 5 minutes per side. Using tongs, transfer the chicken to a plate.

Add the onions, garlic, carrots, fennel, and fennel fronds to the pan and sauté over medium heat until the onions are soft, 5 to 6 minutes. Add the wine, bring to a simmer, and cook to reduce by half. Add the chicken, tomatoes, tomato paste, red pepper flakes, basil, and thyme and simmer until the wine is reduced further, 5 to 7 minutes. Add the stock and bring to a simmer. Reduce heat to low, cover, and cook until the chicken is tender, 40 to 45 minutes.

Transfer the chicken to a platter. Strain the contents of the pan, reserving the liquid and the vegetables. Return the liquid to the pot, and add the balsamic vinegar and cornstarch mixture. Boil until reduced by half, 8 to 10 minutes. Reduce heat to a simmer. Return the chicken and vegetables to the pan and reheat. Add the minced parsley. Taste the pan sauce and adjust the seasoning. Set aside and keep warm.

1 tablespoon minced fresh thyme,
or 1/2 tablespoon dried thyme

4 cups low-salt chicken stock

1 tablespoon balsamic vinegar

1 teaspoon cornstarch mixed with
1 teaspoon cold water

1/2 cup minced fresh flat-leaf parsley,
plus sprigs for garnish

8 ounces rigatoni pasta

Shaved Parmesan for garnish

In a large pot of salted boiling water, cook the pasta until al dente, about 10 minutes. Drain.

To serve, divide the pasta among warmed shallow bowls and top with the chicken and pan sauce. Garnish with parsley sprigs and sprinkle with Parmesan shavings. Serve immediately.

~Serves 6 as an entrée~

Fettuccine with Braised Duck, Fennel, Jerusalem Artichokes, Olives, and Porcini

Recommended wine:
Sangiovese or Chianti Classico

Alternative wine:
Pinot Noir

There is no better way to alleviate the chill of winter than with a hearty braised duck dish. This recipe, full of lusty Mediterranean flavors, relies on a robust red wine and aromatic vegetables to coalesce its deep flavors. A fruity, slightly acidic California Sangiovese or Sangiovese-based Italian Chianti Classico is a good contrast.

2 duck breast halves

2 duck leg-thigh pieces

Kosher salt and freshly ground pepper

4 tablespoons olive oil

2 leeks (white part only), rinsed and sliced

2 cloves garlic, minced

2 carrots, peeled and chopped

1 fennel bulb, trimmed, cored, and thinly sliced

8 ounces small Jerusalem artichokes, scrubbed and trimmed

2 tablespoons minced fresh rosemary, plus sprigs for garnish

1 1/4 cups dry red wine, preferably Sangiovese based

1 1/2 cups low-salt chicken stock

2 tablespoons balsamic vinegar

One 28-ounce can chopped tomatoes with juice

Preheat the oven to 350°F. Sprinkle the duck with salt and pepper on both sides. In a large Dutch oven or flameproof casserole over medium heat, sear the duck (start the breasts skin-side down) 5 to 6 minutes on each side, or until browned. Transfer the duck to a platter. Pour off all the fat from the pan.

Add 2 1/2 tablespoons of the olive oil to the same pan and heat over medium heat. Add the leeks, garlic, carrots, fennel, artichokes, and minced rosemary and sauté until the leeks begin to brown. Add the wine and stir to scrape up the browned bits from the bottom of the pan. Simmer the wine for 3 to 4 minutes. Add the stock, vinegar, tomatoes, tomato paste, olives, and mushrooms, and simmer for another 2 minutes. Return the duck pieces to the pan.

Cover the pan, put it in the oven, and cook until the duck is fork-tender, about 1 1/2 hours. Remove the duck from the pan and let it cool to the touch. Pull the leg meat away from the bone and discard the bones. Cut the breast meat into chunks. Spoon the fat from the pan liquid. Bring the liquid to a simmer and cook to reduce by half. Return the duck to the pan. Set aside and keep warm.

CONTINUED

CONTINUED

Fettuccine with Braised Duck, Fennel, Jerusalem Artichokes, Olives, and Porcini (CONTINUED)

2 tablespoons tomato paste

1/4 cup pitted kalamata olives

1/4 ounce dried porcini mushrooms, soaked in warm water for 30 minutes and drained

1 pound dried fettuccine

Freshly grated Parmesan for garnish

In a large pot of salted boiling water, cook the fettuccine until al dente, 7 to 9 minutes. Drain. Return the fettuccine to the pot, add the remaining 1 1/2 tablespoons olive oil, and toss to coat.

To serve, divide the fettuccine among warmed shallow bowls. Divide the duck and liquid pan sauce evenly over the pasta. Sprinkle with Parmesan and garnish with rosemary sprigs.

~Serves 4 as an entrée~

Osso Buco with Lentils and Wheat Berries

Recommended wine:
Chardonnay

Alternative wine:
Viognier

As the weather begins to cool, I start to think about the aromas and flavors of braised meats and vegetables. Christopher Gross, of Christopher's Fermier Brasserie in Phoenix, Arizona, was the source for this recipe to take the chill off winter. White wine is used to deglaze the vegetables and as an ingredient in the braising liquid for the meaty veal shanks. Have your butcher cut the shanks into slices. A full-bodied Chardonnay is a good match with this nourishing dish.

6 veal shanks cut into crosswise slices about 2 inches thick (about 3 1/4 pounds total)

Kosher salt and freshly ground pepper

3 tablespoons olive oil

2 carrots, peeled and diced

2 stalks celery, diced

1 onion, diced

5 cloves garlic, minced

3 tablespoons minced fresh thyme, or 1 1/2 tablespoons dried thyme

3 tablespoons chopped fresh basil, or 1 1/2 tablespoons dried basil

3 tablespoons minced fresh flat-leaf parsley, plus sprigs for garnish

1 1/2 cups dry white wine

4 tomatoes, seeded (see note, page 68)

1 bay leaf

Season the veal with salt and pepper. In a large Dutch oven or flameproof casserole, heat the olive oil over medium heat until it simmers. Add the veal slices and brown on both sides. You may need to do this in 2 batches, depending on the size of your pan. Using tongs, transfer the veal to a platter.

Preheat the oven to 350°F. In the same pan, over medium-high heat, sauté the carrots, celery, onion, garlic, thyme, basil, and minced parsley for 6 to 7 minutes. Add the wine. Simmer for several minutes. Add the tomatoes and bay leaf. Return the veal to the pan and add the stock. Cover and braise in the oven until the veal is very tender, about 1 1/2 hours.

Bring a small saucepan of salted water to a boil and add the wheat berries. Reduce heat to a simmer, cover, and cook until tender, about 1 hour. Bring another small saucepan of salted water to a boil, add the lentils, reduce heat to a simmer, and cook until tender, 30 to 35 minutes. Drain both and reserve.

1 1/2 cups low-salt chicken or veal
stock

1/2 cup wheat berries (available
from natural foods stores)

1/2 cup green lentils

1 teaspoon cornstarch mixed with
1 teaspoon cold water

Grated lemon zest for garnish

Transfer the veal to a platter and cover loosely with aluminum foil.
Strain the sauce into a saucepan and discard the vegetables. Whisk
in the cornstarch mixture and cook to reduce the sauce by about
half. Taste and adjust the seasoning. Stir in the lentils and wheat
berries.

To serve, divide the osso buco among 6 warmed plates and top with
the sauce, lentils, and wheat berries. Garnish with parsley sprigs and
lemon zest.

~Serves 6 as an entrée~

Curried Lamb Shanks

Recommended wine:
Pinot Noir

Alternative wine:
Syrah/Shiraz

This intensely flavorful lamb dish is highlighted by the use of curry, fresh ginger, star anise, and hot chili. The long braising process infuses the lamb with a beguiling fragrance and flavor intensity. Paired with an aromatic fruit-forward Pinot Noir, the dish reaches a new crescendo. Serve it with couscous or Shiitake Mushroom Risotto with Lemongrass and Ginger (page 97).

1 1/2 tablespoons flour

3 tablespoons Madras curry powder

1/2 teaspoon kosher salt, plus more to taste

1/4 teaspoon freshly ground pepper, plus more to taste

6 lamb shanks (about 4 1/2 pounds total)

1/4 cup olive oil

3 yellow onions, chopped

1 cup chopped carrots

1 tablespoon minced garlic

2 tablespoons minced fresh ginger

1 jalapeño chili, seeded and minced

2 tablespoons minced fresh mint, plus more for garnish

2 tablespoons minced fresh cilantro, plus more for garnish

In a small bowl, combine the flour, 2 tablespoons of the curry powder, the 1/2 teaspoon salt, and the 1/4 teaspoon pepper. Stir to blend. Sprinkle over the lamb shanks to dust them thoroughly.

In a large Dutch oven or large flameproof casserole, heat the oil over medium heat and brown the lamb shanks on all sides in 2 batches. Transfer to a platter. Add the onions, carrots, garlic, ginger, and chili to the pan and sauté until the onions are soft, 7 to 8 minutes. Add the minced mint, minced cilantro, star anise, and mustard seeds and sauté for 2 to 3 minutes.

Add the wine, stock, tomatoes and juice, and lamb shanks and bring to a low simmer. Cover and cook, turning occasionally, until the lamb is tender, about 1 3/4 hours. Transfer the shanks to a platter and cover loosely with aluminum foil, or keep warm in a low oven. Bring the pan liquid to a brisk simmer and cook, uncovered, until well flavored, about 15 minutes. Whisk in the cornstarch mixture and the remaining 1 tablespoon curry powder. Simmer for about 5 minutes. Return the lamb to the pan, cover, and cook until heated through, about 5 minutes. Season with salt and pepper.

To serve, place the shanks on warmed plates and spoon the sauce over. Garnish with the minced mint and cilantro.

~Serves 6 as an entrée~

2 star anise pods

1 teaspoon mustard seeds

1 cup dry red wine

2 $1/2$ cups low-salt lamb, beef, or chicken stock

One 14 $1/2$-ounce can chopped tomatoes with juice

1 teaspoon cornstarch mixed with 1 teaspoon cold water

Braised Beef Short Ribs, Spanish Style

Recommended wine:
Syrah/Shiraz

Alternative wine:
Tempranillo (Spanish Rioja)

This hearty recipe was adapted from one by Heidi Krahling, an inspired chef at Insalata's Restaurant in San Anselmo, California. Chocolate, chipotle chilies, oranges, and sherry add a smoky Spanish depth to the braising liquid. The robust flavors are mirrored by a hearty Syrah/Shiraz or a Spanish Rioja.

3 tablespoons flour

Kosher salt and freshly ground pepper

2 tablespoons olive oil

6 1/2 pounds bone-in beef short ribs, about 2 1/2 inches wide

2 yellow onions, coarsely chopped

1 cup diced carrots

1 cup diced celery

3 cloves garlic, minced

2 canned chipotles en adobo, drained and chopped

1 cup dry red wine

1 cup dry sherry

3 tablespoons tomato paste

One 28-ounce can chopped tomatoes with juice

1 tablespoon minced fresh thyme, or 1/2 tablespoon dried thyme

1 tablespoon dried oregano

1 teaspoon ground cumin

In a small bowl, season the flour with salt and pepper. In a large Dutch oven or flameproof casserole, heat the oil over medium-high heat. Sear the ribs in batches until browned on all sides, turning as needed. Transfer to a platter.

Add the onions, carrots, celery, garlic, and chipotles to the same pot and sauté until lightly browned, about 5 minutes.

Preheat the oven to 325°F. Add the red wine and sherry to the vegetables and cook over high heat, stirring frequently, to reduce by half. Stir in the tomato paste, tomatoes and juice, thyme, oregano, cumin, cinnamon, and bay leaf. Add the ribs and stock to the pan. Bring to a boil, cover, put in the oven, and braise until the meat pulls away from the bone, about 3 hours. Transfer the meat to a platter. Spoon off the fat from the pan liquid.

2 teaspoons ground cinnamon

1 bay leaf

5 cups low-salt beef or chicken stock

1 ounce unsweetened chocolate, chopped

Grated zest of 1 orange

Juice of 2 oranges

1/2 cup packed brown sugar

1 teaspoon cornstarch mixed with
1 teaspoon cold water

GARNISH

1/4 cup minced fresh cilantro

1/2 cup chopped peanuts

Cook the pan liquid over medium-high heat to reduce by a third. Add the chocolate, half the orange zest, the orange juice, brown sugar, and cornstarch mixture. Season to taste.

Return the ribs to the pan and simmer for about 5 minutes to heat through. Serve over pasta or rice in large soup bowls, either on the bone or with the meat removed. Garnish with the remaining orange zest, the cilantro, and chopped peanuts.

~Serves 6 as an entrée~

Braised Short Ribs with Leeks and Green Peas

Bradley Ogden of Lark Creek Inn in Larkspur, California, and One Market in San Francisco has been conjuring up tasty, hearty food for several decades. This adaptation of a recipe from Ogden's *Breakfast, Lunch, and Dinner* combines creamy leeks and green peas with rich, meaty short ribs. A fruity Pinot Noir helps to counterbalance the intensity, while a Merlot offers a pleasing, fruit-forward softness.

Recommended wine:
Pinot Noir

Alternative wine:
Merlot

2 1/2 pounds bone-in beef short ribs

2 tablespoons canola oil

1/4 cup chopped yellow onion

1/4 cup chopped carrot

Kosher salt and freshly ground pepper

1/4 cup chopped celery

2 cloves garlic, minced

Leaves from 4 sprigs thyme, or 1/4 teaspoon dried thyme

1/2 bay leaf

2 to 3 cups low-salt beef stock

1 cup Pinot Noir wine

One 14-ounce can chopped tomatoes with juice

4 large leeks (white part only), halved lengthwise and rinsed

3 tablespoons unsalted butter

1 cup heavy cream

1/4 cup water

1 cup fresh or frozen green peas

Trim the excess fat from the short ribs. In a large Dutch oven or heavy flameproof casserole, heat the oil over medium heat. Add the short ribs and brown them on all sides. Add the onion and carrot and cook for 5 minutes. Season with salt and pepper. Add the celery, garlic, thyme, and bay leaf. Add 2 cups of the stock, the wine, and tomatoes and juice. Reduce heat to a simmer, cover, and cook until the meat is tender, 1 1/2 to 2 hours. As the liquid evaporates during the cooking, add the remaining 1 cup stock, if needed.

Meanwhile, cut the leeks into 1/8-inch-thick slices, yielding about 3 cups. In a large sauté pan or skillet, melt 2 tablespoons of the butter over medium heat until it foams. Add the leeks and cook until wilted, 3 to 4 minutes. Add the cream and season with salt and pepper. Simmer over low heat until the leeks are tender, 10 to 12 minutes. Set aside.

Transfer the short ribs to a platter. Cover loosely with aluminum foil. Spoon the fat from the pan liquid and simmer the liquid until well flavored, 7 to 8 minutes. Strain into a saucepan, set aside, and keep warm.

In a small saucepan, bring the water to a simmer and simmer the peas with the remaining 1 tablespoon butter for 2 minutes, or until just tender. Drain and season with salt and pepper.

To serve, divide the leeks among 4 warm plates. Place the short ribs on top. Sprinkle the peas over the short ribs and pour the sauce around the leeks.

~Serves 4 as an entrée~

Side Dishes

Even in a book about cooking with wine, there comes a place for dishes made without it.

    This chapter offers some of my favorite non-wine-based side dishes, designed to complement the entrées in the book. Despite wine's versatility and unique powers, too much wine in a meal can become tiring to the palate. It can also turn some green vegetables gray because of its acidity.

    A side dish should complement the entrée and create balance in the menu. Many vegetables, grains, and starches accomplish this superbly. Side dishes should also support the entrée by offering a simple, fresh counterpoint to a more complex dish. Vegetable side dishes are a perfect way to add color and texture to a plate. In general, savory, slightly sweet, and sometimes spicy flavors in side dishes help to balance the flavor of wine.

SIDE DISHES

Roasted Prosciutto-Wrapped Radicchio with Radishes and Lemon–Sour Cream Dressing

Recommended wine:
Viognier

Alternative wine:
Sauvignon/Fumé Blanc

Bitter, salty, and tart flavors commingle in this tantalizing first course, providing an ideal showcase for an exotic Viognier or a crisp, tart New Zealand Sauvignon Blanc. I like to serve this dish before seafood entrées. The combination of hot and cold elements in this dish is pleasing.

LEMON–SOUR CREAM DRESSING

1 1/2 cups regular or low-fat sour cream

1 tablespoon white wine vinegar

Grated zest of 1 lemon

1 1/2 tablespoons fresh lemon juice

2 tablespoons horseradish mustard or Dijon mustard

2 tablespoons milk

1 tablespoon honey

2 tablespoons finely chopped green onion, including light green parts

1/4 teaspoon kosher salt

1/8 teaspoon freshly ground pepper

Several drops of Tabasco sauce

3 small heads radicchio, rinsed, cored, and halved

6 ounces thinly sliced prosciutto

5 ounces mixed salad greens

1 1/2 bunches red radishes, trimmed and sliced

TO MAKE THE DRESSING: In a small bowl, combine all the ingredients and whisk thoroughly. Cover and refrigerate.

Preheat the oven to 375°F. Carefully wrap each radicchio half with 2 pieces of prosciutto, covering as much of the radicchio as possible. Place on a baking sheet. Put 2 to 3 toothpicks in each piece to hold the prosciutto closed. Roast for 15 minutes.

To serve, evenly divide the greens among salad plates and place the radishes around the perimeter of each plate. Place 1 radicchio half in the center of each plate. Spoon the dressing over the top and lightly around the edges.

~Serves 6 as a first course~

Goat Cheese and Roasted-Garlic Timbales

An adaptation of a recipe by Kathy Cary, the dynamic chef at Lilly's restaurant in Louisville, Kentucky, this savory side dish is the perfect complement to Smoked Pork Tenderloins with Roasted-Plum Jam (page 131) or other grilled meat and poultry dishes. It can also be served as a first course on top of mixed greens.

Recommended wine:
**See recommendations
for main course**

Alternative wine:
Sauvignon/Fumé Blanc

Purée from 1 head roasted garlic
(note, page 33)

12 ounces fresh white goat cheese

2 eggs

2 egg yolks

1 cup half-and-half, or 1/2 cup half-and-half and 1/2 cup heavy cream

Kosher salt and freshly ground white pepper

Oil-packed sun-dried tomatoes, julienned, for garnish

Preheat the oven to 375°F. In a blender or food processor, process the garlic purée until creamy. Add the goat cheese, eggs, and egg yolks and process until well combined. Add the half-and-half or cream mixture and season with salt and pepper.

Butter 6 to 8 standard muffin cups and pour in the mixture. Place the muffin pan in a roasting pan and add hot water to come halfway up the side of the pan. Place in the oven and bake until the timbales begin to turn golden on top, 30 to 40 minutes. Remove from the oven and let cool slightly.

To serve, carefully unmold the timbales by running a small knife around the edges of each one. Carefully invert onto warmed plates. Sprinkle sun-dried tomatoes over the top.

~Serves 6 to 8 as a first course or side dish~

Maytag Blue Cheese Polenta Cylinders

Recommended wine:
See recommendations for main course

Jimmy Schmidt of the Rattlesnake Club in Detroit, Michigan, one of the heartland's finest chefs, offers this flavorful polenta side dish to accompany a wide variety of meat, game, and poultry entrées. Try it with Rack of Lamb with Hazelnut, Roasted Garlic, and Thyme Crust and Merlot Essence (page 128).

2 1/2 cups water

1 cup milk

3/4 teaspoon kosher salt

1/2 teaspoon freshly ground pepper

2 cups quick-cooking polenta

1/2 cup minced fresh chives

1/2 cup finely grated Parmesan cheese

8 ounces Maytag or other blue cheese

1/4 cup olive oil

In a large saucepan, combine the water, milk, salt, and pepper. Bring to a simmer over medium-high heat, then gradually whisk in the polenta. Reduce heat to medium-low and stir with a spatula or wooden spoon until the polenta is thick enough to allow the spoon to stand up in it, 7 to 8 minutes. Add the chives, Parmesan, and blue cheese and continue to stir until the cheese has melted, 6 to 7 minutes. Taste and adjust the seasoning.

With a spatula, press the polenta mixture into 8 lightly oiled 6-ounce soufflé cups. Smooth and level the surface, pressing down gently to create a flat top. Cover with plastic wrap and refrigerate until firm, about 4 hours.

Preheat the oven to 325°F. Remove the cylinders from the refrigerator and remove the plastic wrap. Invert the soufflé cups to unmold. In a large nonstick skillet, heat the olive oil over medium-high heat. Carefully add the polenta and cook until seared, lightly browned, about 2 minutes on each side. Transfer to paper towels to drain.

Transfer the cylinders to an oiled baking sheet. Bake for 10 to 15 minutes, or until heated through. Serve at once.

~Serves 8 as a side dish~

Roasted-Garlic and Horseradish Mashed Potatoes

I love horseradish and the sweet, nutty flavor of roasted garlic. They are extremely compatible bedfellows when combined with sweet Yukon Gold potatoes oozing with butter. This is a terrific side dish for many of the wine-based dishes in this book.

Recommended wine:
See recommendations for main course

3 1/2 pounds Yukon Gold or red potatoes

1 garlic head roasted (see note, page 33)

2 tablespoons horseradish sauce

2 tablespoons minced fresh thyme, or 1 tablespoon dried thyme

1/2 cup whole milk

6 tablespoons unsalted butter

Chicken stock as needed

Kosher salt and freshly ground pepper

In a large pot of salted boiling water, cook the potatoes until very tender, about 30 minutes. Drain, let cool slightly, and peel the potatoes. In a blender or food processor, process the potatoes in batches until almost smooth. Add the roasted garlic, horseradish, and thyme. Pulse to blend.

Transfer the potatoes to a large saucepan. Place over low heat and stir in the milk and butter. Thin with chicken stock, if necessary. Season with salt and pepper. Serve now, or keep warm in a low oven for up to 30 minutes.

~Serves 6 to 8 as a side dish~

Gorgonzola and Shiitake Bread Pudding

This savory bread pudding is a rich and robust accompaniment to simple meat and poultry entrées. The wine pairing will vary, depending on the selection of entrée. With meat courses, Cabernet Sauvignon will shine, while the delicacy of Pinot Noir will superbly partner with roasted or grilled chicken. This also makes a tasty brunch or lunch entrée by itself.

Recommended wine:
See recommendations for main course

6 slices sourdough French bread

6 tablespoons unsalted butter at room temperature

1 yellow onion, thinly sliced

12 ounces shiitake mushrooms, stemmed and chopped

2 teaspoons dried thyme

1/4 teaspoon kosher salt

4 ounces Gorgonzola cheese, crumbled

2 eggs

1 cup whole milk

1/4 teaspoon freshly ground pepper

Green parts of 1 green onion, finely chopped

Preheat the oven to 300°F. Lightly toast the bread. Divide the butter in half and use half of it to spread on both sides of each bread slice.

In a large sauté pan or skillet, melt the remaining butter over medium-high heat. Add the onion, mushrooms, thyme, and salt and sauté until the onion is soft, about 10 minutes. In a medium bowl, combine the Gorgonzola, eggs, milk, and pepper. Stir to blend.

Butter an 8-inch square baking dish. Place half of the bread in the dish and cover with half of the onion and mushroom mixture, followed by half of the cheese mixture. Add the remaining bread and top with the remaining onion and mushroom mixture, followed by the remaining cheese mixture. Cover with aluminum foil and bake for 1 hour. Remove and reserve the foil. Increase the oven temperature to 350°F and continue baking for 10 minutes, or until lightly browned. Cover with the reserved foil to keep warm until ready to serve.

Sprinkle with the green onion and cut into portions to serve.

~Serves 6 as a side dish, 4 as an entrée~

Desserts and Drinks

Wine and its versatile derivatives have an important place in the creation of decadent, wonderful desserts, though liqueurs such as crème de menthe and crème de cacao are more commonly used in sweet dishes.

Both dry wines—usually reduced, with a little sugar or honey added—and dessert wines, such as Muscat, late-harvest Riesling, and Gewürztraminer, Champagne, port, and Madeira, add a tantalizing flavor note to desserts. Fruit-driven wines, such as Champagne, Muscat, late-harvest Riesling, and Gewürztraminer, are naturals with fruit-based desserts.

While the flavor and acidity of wine can enliven a dessert, at this point in the meal the attention should be on the sweetness of the dessert, not the wine used in it. In this final act of the meal, wine plays an important supporting role.

This chapter also includes two wine-based drinks, "Fire and Ice," a unique beverage created by my colleague, John Ash, for one of our special events at Fetzer Vineyards, and Hot Mulled "Touchdown" Shiraz. They will add enjoyment to summer and winter social occasions respectively. Have fun with them.

DESSERTS AND DRINKS

Drunken Chocolate Cake with Port

Recommended wine:
Port

Emily Luchetti, superstar pastry chef at Farallon in San Francisco and author of the masterful *Stars Desserts,* conjures up some delicious and decadent desserts. This cake is "drunken" because it calls for a good jolt of port, which adds to its intensity. Because of the amount of port in the recipe, this dish doesn't require a dessert wine.

CAKE

6 ounces bittersweet chocolate, coarsely chopped

2/3 cup (1 1/4 sticks) unsalted butter

2/3 cup port

4 large eggs, separated

1 cup plus 4 tablespoons sugar

1 cup all-purpose flour

Pinch of salt

TO MAKE THE CAKE: Preheat the oven to 350°F. Line the bottom of a 9-inch round cake pan with a round of parchment paper. In a double boiler over simmering water, combine the chocolate, butter, and port. Heat, stirring occasionally, until smooth. Set aside and let cool to lukewarm.

Combine the egg yolks and 1/2 cup plus 3 tablespoons of sugar in the bowl of an electric mixer. With the whisk attachment, whip the mixture on high speed until thick, about 3 minutes. Decrease the speed to medium-low and stir in the chocolate mixture. Stir in the flour and salt.

In a large bowl, beat the egg whites with the clean whisk attachment at medium speed until frothy. Increase the speed to high and beat until soft peaks form. Add the remaining 1/2 cup and 1 tablespoon sugar and continue beating until stiff, glossy peaks form. Stir one-third of the egg white mixture into the chocolate batter. Gently fold in the remaining whites. Pour the batter into the prepared pan. Bake until a skewer inserted in the center comes out clean, 30 to 35 minutes. Remove from the oven, let cool, and unmold.

GLAZE

1 cup heavy cream

8 ounces bittersweet chocolate, chopped

CHANTILLY CREAM

2 1/4 cups heavy cream (not ultra-pasteurized)

1 teaspoon vanilla extract

1 1/2 tablespoons sugar

Small pinch of salt

TO MAKE THE GLAZE: In a heavy saucepan, bring the cream to a boil over high heat. Remove from heat and whisk in the chocolate until smooth. Let cool to room temperature and frost the sides and top of the cake. Let the cake stand for at least 1 hour before cutting.

ONE HOUR BEFORE SERVING, MAKE THE CREAM: In a large stainless-steel bowl, combine the cream, vanilla, sugar, and salt. Beat with a whisk just until it holds its shape. Refrigerate until ready to use. Whisk a few more times before serving.

To serve, cut the cake into slices with a knife dipped into hot water and dried. Dollop Chantilly cream on each piece.

~Makes one 9-inch cake; serves 8 to 10~

Spiced Berry "Martinis" with Pinot Noir Syrup and Star Anise Ice Cream

Recommended wine:
Port

Alternative wine:
Late-harvest Zinfandel

An unusual and tasty dessert adapted from a recipe by chef Robert Waggoner of the Charleston Grill in Charleston, South Carolina, this mélange of berries is served with a spiced Pinot Noir syrup. A robust port or late-harvest Zinfandel will stand up to the sweet berry flavors and star anise ice cream.

STAR ANISE ICE CREAM

1 cup whole milk

5 star anise pods

5 egg yolks

1 cup sugar

1 cup heavy cream

PINOT NOIR SYRUP

1 bottle Pinot Noir wine

2/3 cup sugar

1 orange slice

1 thin lemon slice

4 white peppercorns

1 whole clove

1/2 vanilla bean, split lengthwise

1/2 cinnamon stick

4 cups mixed fresh blueberries, raspberries, or blackberries

Mint sprigs for garnish

TO MAKE THE ICE CREAM: In a small saucepan, combine the milk and star anise. Bring to a simmer over medium heat, reduce heat to low, and cook for 5 minutes.

Prepare an ice bath. In a medium bowl, combine the egg yolks and sugar. Gradually whisk in about 1/2 cup of the hot mixture and return to the saucepan. Whisk constantly over medium heat until the mixture coats the back of a spoon. Remove from heat and set the pan in the ice bath. Let cool to room temperature. Strain and discard the star anise. Whisk in the heavy cream. Cover and refrigerate for 2 hours. Freeze in an ice cream maker according to the manufacturer's instructions.

TO MAKE THE SYRUP: Combine all the ingredients in a medium stainless-steel saucepan. Bring to a simmer over medium heat and cook until reduced to a syrupy consistency. Strain and let cool.

To serve, divide the berries among shallow bowls. Top with a scoop of anise ice cream. Drizzle the syrup over and garnish with mint sprigs.

~*Serves 6*~

Port-Poached Pears with Cloves, Cinnamon, and Vanilla

The taste of fresh pears poached in port is truly sublime, particularly when accented by cloves and cinnamon with a layering of intense vanilla. The pears burst with flavor in this simple, tasty dessert. Enjoy it while sipping a little port or Madeira for good measure.

Recommended wine:
Port

Alternative wine:
Madeira

2 cups ruby or tawny port or Madeira

1/2 cup sugar

3/4 cup water

4 cloves

1 stick cinnamon

1 vanilla bean, split lengthwise

3 firm Bosc or Anjou pears, peeled, halved, and cored

1/2 teaspoon cornstarch mixed with 1/2 teaspoon cold water, as needed

Sweetened whipped cream, 6 hazelnut biscotti, and 6 mint sprigs for garnish

In a large stainless-steel saucepan, combine the port or Madeira, sugar, water, cloves, cinnamon, and vanilla bean. Bring to a boil, stirring to dissolve the sugar. Reduce heat and simmer for 10 minutes. Add the pears and simmer until tender, 23 to 25 minutes, turning once. Using a slotted spoon, transfer the pears to a plate.

Simmer the syrup to reduce it by about half, 7 to 8 minutes. If necessary to thicken further, whisk in the cornstarch mixture and simmer for 1 to 2 minutes. Strain the syrup.

To serve, place a pear on each plate. Top with sauce and a dollop of whipped cream. Angle a biscotti on the side of each pear and garnish with a mint sprig.

~Serves 6~

Orange Chiffon Cake with Sangría Compote

Recommended wine:
Muscat or Moscato

Alternative wine:
Riesling

This recipe, adapted from one by Jacky Robert at Maison Robert in Boston, Massachusetts, transforms a Spanish drink into a delicious wine sauce to spoon over an orange cake. A slightly sweet Muscat or late-harvest Riesling is a lovely accompaniment.

SANGRÍA COMPOTE

1 1/2 cups Pinot Noir or Grenache wine

1 1/2 cups Riesling wine

1/4 cup granulated sugar mixed with 1 tablespoon cornstarch

Juice of 1 lime

3/4 cup fresh orange juice

1 cup fresh raspberries

1 cup fresh strawberries, hulled and quartered

4 ripe plums, pitted and cut into wedges

TO MAKE THE COMPOTE: In a large stainless-steel pot, combine the wines, the sugar mixture, and juices. Bring to a boil over high heat, then reduce heat to a simmer. Cook until slightly thickened. In a large bowl, combine the raspberries, strawberries, and plums. Pour the hot liquid over and stir thoroughly. Let cool, then cover and refrigerate.

TO MAKE THE CAKE: Preheat the oven to 350°F. In a large bowl, combine the flour, sugar, baking powder, and salt and stir well. Beat in the oil, orange zest and juice, vanilla, and egg yolks until smooth.

In a large bowl, beat the egg whites and cream of tartar until stiff, glossy peaks form. Stir one-fourth of the egg white mixture into the batter; then gently fold in the remaining egg white mixture. Spoon the batter into an ungreased 10-inch tube pan, smoothing the top. Break any air pockets by cutting through the batter with a knife. Bake until the cake springs back when lightly touched, about 25 minutes. Invert the pan and let the cake cool for at least 40 minutes.

ORANGE CHIFFON CAKE

1 cup sifted cake flour

1/2 cup granulated sugar

1 teaspoon baking powder

1/8 teaspoon kosher salt

2 tablespoons canola oil

1 tablespoon grated orange zest

1/4 cup fresh orange juice

1 teaspoon vanilla extract

2 egg yolks

6 egg whites at room temperature

1/4 teaspoon cream of tartar

Confectioners' sugar for dusting

Mint sprigs for garnish

Loosen the cake from the sides of the pan using a narrow metal spatula or knife. Unmold the cake onto a plate and dust with confectioners' sugar.

To serve, cut the cake into 8 slices. Spoon the compote over the top and side of each slice and garnish with a mint sprig.

~Makes one 10-inch cake; serves 8~

Apple, Grape, and Madeira Clafoutis

Inspired by my colleague, John Ash, who has a love for clafoutis—a delicious French puddinglike dessert—this recipe offers delicious fall fruits in pleasing combination with Madeira, a dessert wine that adds a complex flavor note. A Muscat de Frontignan also pairs quite well.

Recommended wine:
Madeira

Alternative wine:
Muscat de Frontignan

1/2 cup granulated sugar

2 eggs

5 tablespoons unsalted butter, melted

1 cup all-purpose flour

3 tablespoons Madeira or Muscat de Frontignan wine

1 teaspoon grated orange zest

2 teaspoons ground cinnamon

1 cup half-and-half or whole milk

2 cups thinly sliced tart apples, preferably Pippin or Granny Smith

2 cups seedless red grapes, halved

Confectioners' sugar for dusting

Lightly sweetened whipped cream for garnish

With an electric mixer or in a blender, beat the sugar and eggs together at high speed until thick and lemon colored, about 3 minutes. Beat in 4 tablespoons of the melted butter, then the flour, wine, zest, cinnamon, and half-and-half or milk. Let rest for 5 minutes.

Preheat the oven to 375°F. Butter a 9-inch round or square baking dish with the remaining 1 tablespoon of butter. Add the apples and grapes. Pour the batter over the fruit. Bake until the top is golden brown, lightly puffed, and set, 40 to 45 minutes.

Serve warm, with a dusting of confectioners' sugar and a dollop of whipped cream.

~Serves 6 to 8~

Dried Apricot and Muscat Cheesecake in a Gingersnap Crust

Recommended wine:
Muscat or Italian Moscato

Alternative wine:
Gewürztraminer

Being a fan of dried apricots, I try to find almost any way to use them, but the credit for this dessert belongs to my wife, Suzanne. A gentle simmering in fruity Muscat or Gewürztraminer gives them an even more beguiling flavor. Serve the dish with a few sips of Muscat or a late-harvest Gewürztraminer to heighten the apricot flavor.

GINGERSNAP CRUST

2 tablespoons unsalted butter

1 1/2 cups gingersnap cookie crumbs

2 cups (10 ounces) dried apricots

1 cup Muscat, Moscato, or Gewürztraminer wine, plus 3 tablespoons

Three 8-ounce packages regular or low-fat cream cheese at room temperature

3/4 cup sugar, plus 1 tablespoon

2 large eggs

3 egg whites

1 cup regular or reduced-fat sour cream

3/4 cup apricot jam

Edible flowers for garnish (optional)

TO MAKE THE CRUST: Melt the butter in a small saucepan. In a small bowl, combine the cookie crumbs and butter and mix thoroughly. Press evenly over the bottom and slightly up the sides of a 9-inch cheesecake or spring-form pan with a removable rim. Set aside.

Reserve 8 apricot halves. Add the remaining apricots to a medium stainless-steel saucepan along with the 1 cup wine and bring to a boil. Reduce heat to a simmer, cover, and cook until the apricots have plumped, about 15 minutes. Remove from heat and set aside.

Preheat the oven to 350°F. In a blender or food processor, combine the apricot mixture with the 3 tablespoons wine, the cream cheese, the 3/4 cup sugar, the eggs, and egg whites. Purée until smooth. Scrape into the prepared crust. Bake on the center rack of the oven until the cake is set except for the center, which should move slightly when jiggled, 30 to 35 minutes. Remove from the oven, leaving the oven on.

In a small bowl, mix the sour cream with the 1 tablespoon sugar. Spread gently over the top of the cake and return to the oven for 5 to 6 minutes. Remove from the oven and run a thin-bladed cake knife between the pan rim and cake to prevent sticking. Let cool completely. Refrigerate, uncovered, for at least 2 hours. Remove from the refrigerator and release the sides of the pan.

In a small saucepan melt the apricot jam over medium heat, stirring often. Press the jam through a sieve and discard the solids. Spoon the jam onto the cheesecake and spread to evenly coat the top. Refrigerate for 10 to 15 minutes to allow the jam to set.

To serve, arrange the reserved apricot halves decoratively around the outer rim of the cake. Decorate the cake with edible flowers, if desired.

~Makes one 9-inch cake; serves 10~

Peach and Champagne Sorbet

Recommended wine:
Champagne

The Bellini, a mixture of Champagne and puréed white peaches, was made famous by Harry's Bar in Venice. My dear friend and culinary maven Joyce Goldstein invented this dessert for her cookbook *The Mediterranean Kitchen*. Serve it with Champagne for good measure.

1 1/2 pounds ripe peaches, plus sliced fresh peaches for garnish

1/2 cup plus 1 tablespoon sugar

1/2 cup water

3 teaspoons grated lemon zest

3/4 cup brut Champagne, plus a bit more for garnishing

2 tablespoons fresh lemon juice

In a pot of boiling water, blanch the peaches for 1 to 2 minutes. Plunge the peaches into ice water. Peel and pit the peaches, then purée in a blender or food processor. You should have about 2 3/4 cups purée. Transfer to a medium bowl.

In a medium saucepan, combine the sugar and water. Bring to a boil over medium heat, stirring to dissolve the sugar. Add 2 teaspoons of the lemon zest and simmer for 2 minutes. Let the syrup stand 10 minutes, then strain it over the peach purée. Stir in the Champagne, lemon juice, and remaining 1 teaspoon zest. Let cool, then refrigerate for 2 hours to chill. Freeze in an ice cream maker according to the manufacturer's instructions.

Serve in a large glass with a few sliced peaches and a splash of Champagne for an ideal summer dessert.

~Makes 1 1/2 pints~

Hot Mulled "Touchdown" Shiraz

In the chill of winter, particularly around the holidays and during football games, hot drinks win out over beer in my house. This citrus-tinged hot mulled wine features ever-so-fruity Shiraz from Australia (or Syrah from California) in a spicy concoction that will cheer you, no matter which team wins.

2 or 3 wide strips orange zest

Juice of 4 large oranges

Juice of 6 tangerines

2 bottles Shiraz or Syrah wine

1 cup sugar or to taste

6 peppercorns

6 cloves

1 cinnamon stick, plus more for garnish

1/4 teaspoon freshly grated nutmeg

Orange slices for garnish

In a large stainless-steel stockpot, combine the zest, juices, wine, sugar, peppercorns, cloves, cinnamon stick, and nutmeg. Bring to a brisk simmer over high heat and stir until the sugar is completely dissolved. Reduce heat to a low simmer and cook for 4 to 5 minutes. Strain into heatproof mugs.

Garnish the mugs with orange slices, cut halfway through so that they will rest on the rim. Add a cinnamon stick to each glass to use as a swizzle.

~Serves 8 to 10~

John Ash's "Fire and Ice"

My colleague, John Ash, is always full of surprises, finding unusual combinations of foods and exercising his incomparable creative energy. This intriguing wine-based drink was originally featured in our book *From the Earth to the Table*, but it deserves an encore here. A spicy, fruity Gewürztraminer or Riesling is essential, as oaked wines simply will not work. The "fire" is in the chilies, while the "ice" is both the ice and the cooling mint. This summer drink is pretty, refreshing, and just plain fun.

2/3 cup sugar

1/2 cup water

2 teaspoons minced jalapeño or serrano chili

2 tablespoons finely chopped yellow bell pepper

2 tablespoons minced fresh mint

1/2 cup fresh lime or lemon juice

2 cups sparkling mineral water

2 cups apple juice

2 cups Gewürztraminer or Riesling wine

Ice cubes for serving

In a large saucepan, combine the sugar and water. Bring to a boil over high heat, stirring until the sugar is dissolved. Remove from heat, stir in the chili, and let cool.

Add the bell pepper, mint, lime or lemon juice, mineral water, apple juice, and wine. Stir thoroughly. Transfer to a pretty pitcher. Pour over ice cubes in wineglasses.

~Serves 6 to 8~

BIBLIOGRAPHY

Andrews, Colman. *Catalan Cuisine*. New York: Atheneum, 1988.

Ash, John, and Sid Goldstein. *From the Earth to the Table*. New York: Dutton, 1995.

Chiarello, Michael. *The Tra Vigne Cookbook*. San Francisco: Chronicle Books, 1999.

Child, Julia, Louisette Berthollel, and Simone Beck. *Mastering the Art of French Cooking*, vol. 1. New York: Alfred A. Knopf, 1979.

Corriher, Shirley. "Less Is Really More When Making Reduction Sauces." *Fine Cooking*, April/May, 1999.

Favorite Recipes of California Winemakers. San Francisco: Wine Advisory Board, 1963.

Feniger, Susan, and Mary Sue Milliken. *City Cuisine*. New York: William Morrow and Company, 1989.

Frost, Doug. "The Way of Sake." *Sante Magazine*, September/October, 1999.

Goldstein, Joyce. *The Mediterranean Kitchen*. New York: William Morrow and Company, 1989.

Goldstein, Sid. *The Wine Lover's Cookbook*. San Francisco: Chronicle Books, 1999.

Harlow, Jay. *Enjoying American Wines*. San Francisco: California Culinary Academy, 1986.

Hébert, Malcolm. *California Wine Lovers' Cookbook*. San Francisco: Wine Institute and Wine Appreciation Guild, 1983.

Heffernan, Kerry, and Tom Kirkman. "Flavoring with a Fortified Favorite." *Sante Magazine*, holiday issue, 1999.

Herbst, Sharon Tyler. *The Food Lover's Tiptionary*. New York: Hearst Books, 1994.

Keller, Thomas, and Mark Ruhlman. "Make the Most out of Marinades." *San Ramon Valley Times*, August 9, 2000.

Kolpan, Steven, Brian H. Smith, and Michael A. Weiss. *Exploring Wine*. Hyde Park, NY: Van Nostrand Reinhold, Culinary Institute of America, 1996.

Lagasse, Emeril. *Every Day's a Party*. New York: William Morrow and Company, 1999.

Luchetti, Emily. *Stars Desserts*. New York: Harper Collins, 1991.

McGee, Harold. *On Food and Cooking*. New York: Collier Books, Macmillan Publishing, 1984.

Ogden, Bradley. *Bradley Ogden's Breakfast, Lunch & Dinner*. New York: Random House, 1991.

Pence, Caprial. *Caprial's Bistro Style Cuisine*. Berkeley: Ten Speed Press, 1998.

Peterson, James. *Sauces*. New York: Van Nostrand Reinhold, 1991.

St. Pierre, Brian. *The Perfect Glass of Wine*. San Francisco: Chronicle Books, 1996.

Studley, Helen. "Versatile Verjus." *Sante Magazine*, September/October, 1999.

Tropp, Barbara. *The Modern Art of Chinese Cooking*. New York: William Morrow and Company, 1982.

INDEX

INDEX

INDEX

INDEX

INDEX

INDEX

INDEX

NOTES

NOTES

NOTES

NOTES

TABLE OF EQUIVALENTS

The exact equivalents in the following tables have been rounded for convenience.

LIQUID/DRY MEASURES

U.S.	METRIC
1/4 teaspoon	1.25 milliliters
1/2 teaspoon	2.5 milliliters
1 teaspoon	5 milliliters
1 tablespoon (3 teaspoons)	15 milliliters
1 fluid ounce (2 tablespoons)	30 milliliters
1/4 cup	60 milliliters
1/3 cup	80 milliliters
1/2 cup	120 milliliters
1 cup	240 milliliters
1 pint (2 cups)	480 milliliters
1 quart (4 cups, 32 ounces)	960 milliliters
1 gallon (4 quarts)	3.84 liters
1 ounce (by weight)	28 grams
1 pound	454 grams
2.2 pounds	1 kilogram

LENGTH

U.S.	METRIC
1/8 inch	3 millimeters
1/4 inch	6 millimeters
1/2 inch	12 millimeters
1 inch	2.5 millimeters

OVEN TEMPERATURE

Fahrenheit	Celsius	Gas
250	120	1/2
275	140	1
300	150	2
325	160	3
350	180	4
375	190	5
400	200	6
425	220	7
450	230	8
475	240	9
500	260	10